FROZEN ASSETS

FROZEN ASSETS

The New Order of Figure Skating

Mark A. Lund

ASHTON INTERNATIONAL MEDIA, INC.

Worcester • New York

ASHTON INTERNATIONAL MEDIA, INC.

Published by Ashton International Media, Inc.
44 Front Street, Suite 280, Worcester, MA 01608

www.ifsmagazine.com

DESIGNED BY MARCUS C. GEMMA

Library of Congress Control Number: 2002114329

ISBN 0-9721402-0-4

This book is dedicated to my mother Eleanor.
For she has always been my guiding light.

Contents

Prologue
1

Dynasty
5

A Star Is Born
21

Lights, Camera, Public
55

The Studios
69

Takeover
95

Skates for Hire
109

It Was All for the Federation
133

Pressures, Perks and Paydays
145

1994
161

Gone with the Gold
187

Michelle Kwan, Inc.
209

Conflict
225

The Verdict Is In
251

Kristi, Scott and a Cast of Thousands
269

Epilogue
283

Index
289

We are each the authors of our own lives...
there is no way to shift the blame
and no one else to accept the accolades.

Paul McGill in *A Woman of Substance*

Prologue
Secret Society

The day began just as the last several had. Rise at 5:30 a.m. to be ready for CNN at 7:00 a.m., and then off to at least a dozen national television appearances—with at least 50 calls a day to Lois Elfman to be briefed on the phone calls she made to the media-forbidden Olympic Village. My last interview was usually at 7:00 p.m. for the NBC affiliates, and then I was off to more events.

I am not the President of the United States, and Lois Elfman is not my Chief of Staff. I am the Publisher of *International Figure Skating*, and Lois Elfman is the Editor in Chief. This was February 2002, and "Skategate" was all everyone was talking about. I didn't attend Olympic figure skating competitions. I attended figure skating "events." Though I watched the skating on the ice, it was immaterial to what was going on in the seats, on the concourse and in the VIP lounges of the Delta Center arena.

I knew then that the sport and art of figure skating would never be the same again after these games. In fact, the drama was only beginning.

Figure skating has always been a secret society of sorts. From the fans' point of view, what you see on the ice and what you are told by the Dick Buttons of the world is generally all you get. If you want to work in this sport—never mind publish the world's largest figure skating magazine—you have to play politics. It is a juggling act more intense than balancing on the quarter-inch steel blade of a skate.

Politics in Washington is nothing compared to politics in figure skating. You can get a law passed faster in the United States Congress than a simple rule can change at the Congress of the International Skating Union.

But now Washington is involved, with the July 31, 2002, arrest of Alimzhan Tokhtakhounov in Italy for conspiring to fix the results of the ice dance and pair competitions at the XIX Olympic Winter Games. I suspect more arrests are on the way and that major players in the sport will be involved in this criminal investigation. It's about time that governments in the United States, France, Italy and Russia are investigating this conspiracy and other dealings in this sport. For too long the powers that be in figure skating have taken advantage of the hard work of the athletes that make this sport one of the greatest.

Figure skating is like a soap opera. Last season's cliffhanger was the ice dance protest at the World Figure Skating Championships in Nagano, Japan, in March. Then we previewed what's to come this season with Tokhtakhounov's arrest in July.

Lights, camera—figure skating.

Although there are hundreds of thousands of skaters and tens of millions of fans throughout the world, the sport is controlled by about a dozen individuals that set the policies for this quarter-of-a-billion dollar industry. Whether they are elected, are power brokers, are made famous by an Olympic win or have proclaimed their own self-importance, they lay the foundation for what, how and when we see this sport.

A lot has changed since Oksana Baiul won Olympic gold in 1994. With a wave of business consolidations and consumer boredom with sameness, the world of professional skating is now all but gone. A studio system now exists, and if you aren't under contract with either International Management Group, the multibillion dollar sports marketing conglomerate, or Tom Collins Enterprises, headed by Tom Collins, the flamboyant owner of *Champions on Ice*, you are, as the movie says, *Home Alone*.

But no other sport radiates glamour and excitement like the sport of figure skating does. Each event carries an aura of Hollywood, with celebrities running to and fro, both meeting and avoiding the public. Some stars are here to stay, but others—careless in their planning and often given bad advice—fall by the wayside and out of favor. The former always make for a nice cover story, but it is the latter that we always want to read about.

Don't let anyone tell you otherwise: while figure skating certainly existed prior to 1994, it was not the living television series that it has been the last eight years.

The greatest cast of stars from yesterday to today was assembled that year in Lillehammer. Their ambitions and their failings led us all on a journey that has been the most celebrated, the most reported, the most admired and the most hated.

In 2002, a new world order for figure skating is in place. The performances are set, the rules are in place and the cameras are on. But is the sport ready to take itself into the 21st century and beyond?

This is the story of the chosen few who guide the dynasty that is figure skating—yesterday, today and tomorrow.

Dynasty

1

"It's great to have a love of your art and craft, but you're not going to be around for long unless you're responsible and have a vision."
– Scott Hamilton, 1984 Olympic
Men's Champion

Dynasty

Once considered merely a genteel pastime, figure skating in the current day is an extensive empire.

This dynasty is controlled by an elite group of individuals who attract the public's attention, rule the sport's direction, receive the most accolades and have the power to banish others from, or admit them to, the kingdom.

These personalities are a discriminating mix of top ice royalty, business titans and one ultimate politician.

The most recognizable member of this elite club is indisputably Scott Hamilton, the 1984 Olympic Men's Champion and co-founder of the *Stars on Ice* tour.

As a performer, Hamilton is the ultimate entertainer, and crowds respond to him like no other. As a commentator for the 2002 Olympics, his utter disbelief over the pair result sparked public outcry. From ice shows, to television broadcasts, to his cancer foundation, his influence is seen over the entire spectrum of the sport and beyond.

With an unbelievable will and drive, Hamilton's agenda generally becomes the law of the skating land.

"When I was coming up as a professional, I decided I wanted to build something. The Olympic Games were something where I was able to share that with my country and my family and the skating world. What I have done as a professional is something purely meant to take me to the next place, where I could touch somebody in a different way," shares Hamilton.

"I think that's important not only to an audience, who gets to see great levels of diversity and innovative dance and art, but also personally, you get to find out who you are, and you get to explore different emotions and depths to yourself."

Speaking about Hamilton, 1984 Olympic Women's silver medalist and former *Stars on Ice* castmate Rosalynn Sumners says, "He's the heart and soul of our sport ... for a lot of reasons. Not just because he's the Olympic Champion or his battle with cancer. It's Personality, Personality, Personality!"

Is the personable Hamilton you see on the ice the real deal? Contends 1976 Olympic Men's bronze medalist Toller Cranston, who also toured with Hamilton, "Yes, Scott Hamilton is the greatest, but he is no saint."

From the time Brian Boitano won the "Battle of the Brians" at the 1988 Calgary Olympics, Boitano has been a guiding force in figure skating. His memorable Olympic performance launched the modern generation of male skaters striving for the complete package of power, technique and artistry.

His influence also shone on the professional front. He raised his level of skating and was a model of quality and consistency. On the business side, his company, White Canvas Productions, has been behind many memorable skating shows of the past decade, and each year he headlines *Brian Boitano's Skating Spectacular,* the skating exhibition that is one of the most watched such events on television.

"Of all the greatest skaters, particularly the greatest professional skaters, why did I have to have the toughest competition in the history of figure skating, with Scott Hamilton and Brian Boitano?" quips a good-natured Brian Orser, two-time Olympic Men's silver medalist, who lost the ultimate title to both men.

"I'm most definitely a fan of Brian's. I'm a fan of mostly his commitment and his drive. It blows me away. From 1988 to a couple years ago, he was driven and gave 100 percent, even in every practice. It was amazing. I'm most impressed with that. He's a machine."

Claims *Stars on Ice* creative director Sandra Bezic, who has worked with Boitano on a number of projects, "Of anyone I've ever worked with, he has the most powerful mental capacity to apply himself, to set a goal and work towards it. He's phenomenal."

Katarina Witt, the two-time Olympic Women's Champion from Germany, possesses selling power normally only associated with American skaters. In nearly two decades on the scene, she has continually reinvented herself through projects that transcend skating—be it acting appearances, a *Playboy* pictorial or speaking out for the right to privacy. When it comes to moves on the ice, she annually headlines shows around the globe. From her made-for-television events in the U.S., like *Divas on Ice*, to her *Summer Night on Ice* shows in Europe, Witt's star gets brighter each year.

It's the combination of sex appeal, the ability to put the audience in the palm of her hand and a strong business sense that have afforded Witt a long, successful reign in the sport.

"I'm a workaholic, and I'm a maniac when it comes to just keeping going. That's what it is. People see that it's honest work, and that I'm not going somewhere to just try and collect a paycheck," states Witt.

"I'm always working hard for it. It's not being only a skater. It's starting my own projects, being a producer and being a spokesperson for them and the sport."

Determines Orser, "She's the most fierce competitor I've ever seen. She can turn it on. Boy, if we could bottle that, we would be super rich!

"She's also a joy, and she's a ham. She likes to have fun, but she's the utmost professional. There are very few team players out there, and Kat is one of them."

The same can be said for Witt's 1992 Olympic successor, Kristi Yamaguchi. Always ready to anchor a television special or give back to worthy causes through her Always Dream Foundation, Yamaguchi brings a golden look to the sport. She served as the goodwill ambassador for the 2002 Olympic Winter Games, and her glowing image has increasingly caught the eye of the corporate world, where she is more in demand than ever for endorsements.

If Witt is skating's queen, Yamaguchi is its picture-perfect princess. Her elegance, work ethic and pride lent both glamour and substance to the *Stars on Ice* tour and pro events for the past decade.

A modest Yamaguchi says she was unaware of the effect her presence had on the growing *Stars on Ice*.

"Oh, not at all," she states. "I thought I was joining a show that already had a great cast. I mean, Scott Hamilton—what more do you need? It was not until just a few years ago when I could look back and see how much the tour had grown, and I grew with it.

"I didn't really see the change while I was doing it. I was just so young and naïve, and tying to fit in as much as possible, and wasn't thinking of much beyond that."

Those around her quickly recognized the effect Yamaguchi had on professional skating.

"She's perfect. Bob (Kain, co-founder of *Stars on Ice* and President and COO, Americas, IMG) has said that he's never seen any athlete, other than Chris Evert in tennis, who has handled the demands put on them with such grace," says Sumners.

Adds former *Stars on Ice* choreographer Lea Ann Miller, "We've all had a bad period in our career, but not Kristi. She's the epitome of a true professional."

"Kristi is one of the most tasteful people in the world. That's why she is a legend," says Boitano.

Yamaguchi's former pair partner, 1996 U.S. Men's Champion Rudy Galindo, says it is her determination that has set her apart.

"Kristi knew she wasn't naturally talented, but she knew skating was what she wanted, so she made up for it with her mental preparedness," Galindo says. "That takes a smart brain. I saw firsthand that she worked so hard and was so determined in her mind to make it."

And, of course, there is Michelle Kwan, the heir apparent, who never quite managed to get the crown. For the past four years, the figure skating world literally revolved around her participation. So convinced of her bankability, sources have said that ABC Sports even paid appearance fees to ensure she was at its events. Now, two Olympics and two stunning losses later, what happens? Do the media, public and skating continue to make the ultimate investment in Kwan? The Walt Disney Company has. They signed her to a multi-year, multi-level agreement in the spring of 2002.

While in many ways Kwan has served as the barometer for skating, she doesn't see things that way. "People from the outside can see that. I don't think I'll ever realize it in that way. Sometimes I think, *Skating is just skating. It's not that big of a deal,*" Kwan says. "I'm just very fortunate. Who knew this would happen in figure skating? I'm always saying, 'This is just entertainment.' It's not like I'm changing the world or anything."

"Whether Michelle won the gold or didn't win the gold, the public is proud of her. She fascinates them, and she is a fighter. The public is with her," states Sumners.

However, Sumners cautions that Kwan needs to be certain of her next step.

"I just think she needs to be a little careful. If she hangs in four more years, the public might go, 'Oh, for Pete's sake.' Not that they are not going to support her, but it is a little bit like with a Mary Decker (Olympic middle distance runner–turned–long distance runner). You have to know when to stay in and when to get out, because of the public support."

Offers Cranston, "Kwan is a great artist, but great artists in the history of art, if they start spinning their wheels, they start losing ground. It is questionable for Kwan whether in the last year she wasn't more spinning her wheels than treading on new territory. It was sort of like, we have seen it before, but we have seen it better."

Beyond those who sparkle on the ice, others who rule the sport are seldom seen in the public eye.

Kenneth Feld, president and CEO of Feld Entertainment, employs the largest number of figure skaters via his *Disney on Ice* tours that play throughout the world and introduce the joy of skating as entertainment to countless families every year.

Tom Collins produces *Champions on Ice*, the tour known for

showcasing the best and brightest Olympic-eligible skaters. Most skaters revere him, while a few fear his wrath. When you fall out of grace with Collins, the chances of getting back into the fold are slim to none.

Then there is sports marketing giant International Management Group (IMG). From the *Stars on Ice* tours, to the impetus behind professional competitions and shows, to sponsorships with governing bodies of eligible skating, IMG's prominence in skating is felt across the board—nowhere more strongly, though, than in the pro arena, where if you want to work, you had better be in the IMG stable or risk being left out in the cold.

Whether you are a skating superstar or looking for a niche, IMG can help you. Case in point: Lucinda Ruh, the Swiss spinning sensation, whose career skyrocketed after she was taken on by IMG, despite her lack of jumping ability or significant competitive resume.

Even prior to signing with IMG, she was welcomed with open arms at the last World Professional Figure Skating Championships in 2000—and some feel judged on another scale.

"She did two single jumps in the short program and beat Surya Bonaly (three-time World silver medalist)," says Liz Manley, the 1988 Olympic Women's silver medalist. "I love Lucinda Ruh, but there's no way I can justify that. This was a competition."

When it comes to exhibition events, sports executive Steve Disson is skating's go-to guy to get the shows on television. He's said to be one of the three people in the United States who undertakes risky time-buys—buying airtime from the networks, producing your own shows and selling sponsorships yourself.

"Scott [Hamilton] calls him 24/7. He's the hardest working guy, hustler, out there for skating. You want him on your side," says Miller, who choreographs and directs many of the Disson events.

"I respect how hard he works to get these shows done, and it makes me want to work that much harder for them. He's a great cheerleader for skating."

Last, but not least, is the venerable president of the International Skating Union (ISU), Ottavio Cinquanta.

If anyone in the sport has the mentality of dictator, it is Cinquanta. Let there be no mistake—while he stresses to the media that he has no real power and that "the ISU Council makes the decisions," eligible skating spins on his ideas, judgments and decisions.

These are the leaders that get the ball rolling and get things done. They are responsible for what is seen on television, on tour and at live events.

As with its rulers, figure skating has no shortage of compelling situations.

Today's eligible skaters are burdened with the pressure of increased technical demands, but they also are reaping the rewards of the instant celebrity culture—not to mention earning a nice living. Some of the brightest North American stars are making money hand-over-fist in competition and on tour.

This is a far cry from how things used to be.

"When I was World Champion (in the late 1980s), I did Tommy Collins' tour for about $200 a show. Maybe my last year I got $250 a show," recalls Orser. "But I thought I had the whole world by the ass, because I had all of these travelers checks that they gave me. I had $2,000 and was thrilled!"

Skaters of Orser's generation had their turn at fortune after the 1994 Winter Olympics, when pro skating was everywhere. Now, it's practically nowhere—at least from the competition standpoint. The World Professional Figure Skating Championships, the U.S. Professional Figure Skating Championships, the Challenge of

Champions and the World Team Championships all have vanished. What brought the joy ride to a screeching halt?

"There were way too many projects out there, way too many skaters saying yes to everything. I really think that it's not the fault of the producers of the projects, but the skaters themselves," offers Boitano. "They didn't have any criteria for saying yes or no. People were just saying yes to everything for the money. The result was a lot of crap on TV. And the public got tired of it."

Adds Sumners, "Obviously, pro skating was oversaturated. I mean, you can only shove something down somebody's throat so much before they say, I have had enough. Also, don't forget, I think the public's attention span is pretty short as far as the entertainment world. And as a professional entity, we are more entertainment than we are sports."

Paul Wylie, 1992 Olympic Men's silver medalist, says it didn't help matters that some of the next generation's brightest skating stars did not seek out competition as a professional.

"What was missing was the way that Kristi Yamaguchi said, 'I will compete against you guys,' and Katarina Witt said, 'Hey, I will skate against Kristi.' It just takes one person in the group to say, 'I am not into that,' to make it go away, because we are too small a group to have exclusivity. You have to train, you have to win, you have to lose—that's all part of it," says Wylie, who did his share of winning and losing during his six-year pro career (before he headed off to Harvard Business School).

Also coming with the territory is the media, which is perhaps skating's greatest friend and enemy, all rolled into one. And nothing would be possible without fans buying tickets to events. Sometimes they want more than just a skating show. They want the inside story on the skaters, making for tricky waters to navigate.

Just ask the top two ladies from Lillehammer—Oksana Baiul

and Nancy Kerrigan. Each has served time as both the media darling and favorite target. In the last eight-and-a-half years, their lives have taken vastly different paths, but each has found what they wanted most—family and stability.

There is also the conundrum of Tara Lipinski. She defeated Kwan for the Olympic title in 1998, at the age of 15, then promptly waved goodbye to eligible competition and joined *Stars on Ice*. What were her real reasons for turning pro?

"Tara came right into the professional world, but I still think there are places she could have gone competitively. I'm not saying it was wrong for her to turn pro, because I'll never say that about anybody. It's just, you wonder what other athletic things that she could have done, having won one World title and one Olympic Games at such an early age," says Hamilton.

Lipinski's career path today is also intriguing. She now primarily skates in the tour and forgoes most special events and competitions. She is turning her sights, instead, to Hollywood.

In the movies is exactly where you would expect to find the dramatic tale of Jamie Salé & David Pelletier at the 2002 Olympic Winter Games in Salt Lake City. The Canadian couple was the apparent victim of a plot by the French and Russian figure skating federations to garner gold for their respective teams in ice dance and pairs. After nearly a week's worth of allegations, admissions and outcries, a second gold medal in pairs was awarded to the Canadians. That remedy sparked a hot debate in the skating world—almost as hot as the controversy itself.

Pair competitor and three-time U.S. Champion John Zimmerman still wonders why the dance aspect of the supposed arrangement wasn't scrutinized at the time.

"I was surprised they even continued to have the ice dance competition, if it was indeed the whole reason for the pairs scandal in the first place," he declares. "How was that event altered? Before the dance took place, they knew about how it was linked to the pairs scandal, but nothing was done about it. It was bizarre. Then, of course, the French team won. It's like, 'Wake the hell up!' Only after the arrest [of reputed mobster Alimzhan Tokhtakhounov] months later is this second half of the deal even being talked about."

The Olympic controversy is only part of the Salé and Pelletier story. After their homecoming skating show, which aired on NBC, the duo all but fell off the face of the earth as far as the general public was concerned. They didn't tour in either the Canadian *Stars on Ice* or the post-Olympic *Champions on Ice*. What happened?

"Their agent (Craig Fenech, who had never before represented skaters) was just pushing way too hard for money. It's not there in skating. We're not in the league of Tiger Woods; we're not NHL athletes. There is great money in figure skating today, but not those kind of salaries," assesses Liz Manley, of Canada.

"I heard they were asking for $30,000 per show," says Tamara Moskvina, the coach of the 2002 Olympic Pair co-Champions Elena Berezhnaya & Anton Sikharulidze.

"When you're the Olympic Champion and at the top of your game, you want to get out there and skate. You want to get out there every night and have them announce you as the Olympic champion. And bask in that feeling, plus collect a paycheck and just enjoy it. They've made some really interesting decisions with where they've gone with their careers," says Canada's four-time World Men's Champion Kurt Browning.

In May, Salé and Pelletier parted ways with Fenech, and they joined *Stars on Ice* for the current season, both in the U.S. and Canada. But many in figure skating feel they messed up, missed their moment in the sun and lost millions.

The Salt Lake judging fiasco had once again rocketed skating from the realm of an elite sport straight to the center of pop culture.

It was considered a welcome adventure by many in the sport, as the back room dealings finally faced the harsh light of day—while others thought it was much ado about next-to-nothing, because that's the nature of the beast called figure skating. Opinions run rampant on what needs to happen, and what doesn't, with the judging system—if anything at all.

"I suppose it did expose what has been going on. I don't know whether it's a bad thing; it's something. Politics are like that. Is everything whiter than white? Is sport whiter than white?" theorizes 1984 Olympic Ice Dance gold medalist Christopher Dean. "It's reality. You try to improve on that.

"Who knows whether people will still be enamored and watch it. Yet people are still going to watch WWF and boxing, for all of those controversial results. So the audience will likely watch, and they will always have their own opinions."

The path chosen next can make all the difference to the success or failure of the journey.

"If skating hasn't done what it's supposed to do, after this Olympics in Salt Lake City when we had an American gold medalist, it's going to be tough," cautions Boitano.

Says long-time skating agent and entrepreneur Michael Rosenberg, who bid his farewell to the sport on the eve of the Olympics, "Skating will always be popular with two to three percent of the North American population, and that's the base on which to build. Half a million to a million people would go to any ice show and watch everything skating on the television; they live or die through the magic of the sport. The question is to try to get back up where we were, which was a base of four to five million people."

Every dynasty falls victim to its own success, as times change along with the people on its throne. Nowhere is that more apparent than in our modern sports culture, with heydays reduced to memorabilia, museums and fans' "What ever happened to?" chats.

Figure skating now wonders who among the next generation will step up to the plate and accept the mantle of responsibility that goes along with it.

Wylie says, "All it will take is a handful of skaters to decide, *You know what, it's time for us to enjoy that time again,* and to make their desire known and follow through."

That is the essence of the dynasty of figure skating.

A Star Is Born

"Why you are a performer is to get your applause, and to be able to emotionally move your audience."

– Katarina Witt,
two-time Olympic Women's gold medalist

A Star Is Born

Talent alone isn't a sure ticket to fame.

As a rule, a skater must combine the necessary credentials with the right looks, personality, story and advisors.

"The difference between a star and an extremely good skater that nobody really thinks about is almost always the connection to an audience and/or that something out of the ordinary has happened to them," declares former skaters' agent Michael Rosenberg.

"For the group who overcame adversity—whether it's cancer, sudden death of a husband, being HIV positive or getting whacked on the knee—the audience never forgets it.

"It's a combination of on-ice accomplishments and off-ice charisma."

23

Two-time Olympic Men's Champion, television commentator and event producer Dick Button says, "Star quality is indefinable. It's a magical something. It can come from anywhere, and it can come out of something else. You can be born with it, or you can develop it."

Indeed, for some, the stardom ride is long-lasting.

Others find it all too fleeting.

How does the star system work? Who are the skaters in it? And what are the constants all luminaries have that helped propel them to the top?

The essence of a skating star is someone who's bigger than life and transcends the sport.

This requires activity beyond the rink to allow the public to see all facets of their personalities.

"You have to broaden your base so that your appeal is not simply skating," declares Olympic bronze medalist, artist and author Toller Cranston. "You have to have a profile."

With the increased presence of television and the media as a whole, the process of establishing a profile starts early and is crucial.

"We are always teaching our students how to become stars," says Tamara Moskvina, coach of 2002 Olympic Pair co-Champions Elena Berezhnaya & Anton Sikharulidze.

"When we start working with skaters, we dig deeply into their skills to take out what they offer. What they have already on the surface, we make it to the extreme. What they don't have and never will have, we try to replace with something else," she elaborates. "It's a big, long, tactical process. It is the development of the complete star."

In skating circles, Moskvina is not only legendary for her accomplished teams, but for her story-spinning, as well.

To hear her tell it, the saga of Elena and Anton is the stuff tragic Russian novels are made of. After Elena was seriously injured when the blade of her then-partner struck her head while training in Riga, Latvia, Anton rushed to Elena's side and ultimately spirited her back in the dead of night to their native St. Petersburg, Russia. Anton and Elena each left their partners to skate together.

The accident, unfortunately, did happen, but the rest ... who's to say? When asked about her coach's storytelling, Elena laughs, "Oh, Tamara and her stories!"

Yet Moskvina knows the media eats up a good tale and that it pushes a skater away from the pack. "Generating publicity and seeking media or advertising opportunities puts a skater on the fast track to becoming famous, so you do what you do," she explains.

Champions on Ice publicity director Lynn Plage agrees. "After a skater starts collecting medals and is moving up that ladder, the media is hungry to find out more about them," she says. "They want to develop more of a personality for their viewers or readers.

"They want to find what makes each skater appealing. Are they interesting people? Is their family interesting? Do they have interests outside of the sport? It's an ongoing process."

How do skaters prepare for this public responsibility?

"Media training is a good idea," states Plage. "It's not changing their personalities, but working *with* their personalities—that they don't give only yes-and-no answers."

Being media savvy is but one critical factor on the path to stardom.

"One needs to be diverse and entertaining, with some sort of emotion," voices 1984 Olympic Ice Dance Champion Christopher Dean.

Five-time World ice dance medalist Shae-Lynn Bourne agrees.

"You can do well competitively and be a World Champion, and, still, no one wants to hire you unless the audience likes you," she notes. "It's not just about the technical elements."

That would explain why 1994 Olympic Men's silver and bronze medalists, Elvis Stojko and Philippe Candeloro, never want for work, while the gold medalist, Alexei Urmanov, stays home.

Because of his rapport with crowds, Scott Hamilton is, for many, skating's supreme performer.

Two beliefs he lives by have cemented Hamilton's winning connection.

"First and foremost, I am there for the audience. They are not there for me," Scott declares. "When I come on the ice, my whole feeling is that I am there for the sole purpose of trying to give something. I am not there to take something. I'm there for the audience; that's the thing I've tried to put first."

Hamilton also gives each performance his all.

"On tour in *Stars on Ice* I would go out every night and give one hundred percent," he says. "Regardless of if I missed every jump, I wouldn't give up on the performance. I always tried to impart that to skaters around me. It's not exactly about what you do. Sometimes it's what people think you do.

"It's about creating an atmosphere of energy and of excitement and of fun that goes beyond what you do in the air in the jumps."

"Scott learned this early on in his pro career, that there are other elements that you have to bring to skating, or else people are going to lose interest after you can no longer do the hardest tricks," explains Paul Wylie, who co-starred with Scott in *Stars on Ice* for six years.

"That is what I admire most about him, the way he continues to create and to energetically pursue these entertainments. And that's what it is to Scott—a piece of entertainment, not just a run through or a program. That's what is so amazing."

On the personal side, Paul fondly refers to Scott as like an older brother, "one whose shadow you can never seem to skate out of.

"He's also a practical joker. And talk about locker room banter! If you came back and you didn't quite hit it, you didn't want to tell Scott. He's also a guy who didn't let anyone in on the secret about his cancer, because he didn't want to cause anybody to fear."

Offers fellow former *Stars on Ice* cast member Kristi Yamaguchi, "On my first day on the tour he was giving me subtle advice here and there that I appreciated. I definitely credit him with the way I've developed as a professional, and the kind of skater I am now."

"Scott makes the audience a part of his performance probably better than anyone," says Byron Allen, vice president of Winter Sports at IMG and producer of *Stars on Ice.*

Scott's long-time publicist, Michael Sterling, recalls an early sign that proved prophetic. "When I first started representing him, which was in 1986, I was sent materials on him, one of which was a promotional tape about Scott that had been made, entitled 'They Don't Make Scott Hamiltons Any More.' That pretty much still says it all," says Sterling.

Scott's unique persona on the ice stems from what he took away from ice shows as a young child, says Sterling. "So many of these skaters look up to—as would be expected—some sort of icon in the sport, like Kristi to Peggy Fleming. But Scott looked up to the people who were the clowns and funny guys he saw on the ice," Sterling notes.

"He had this understanding of what showmanship was about, early on, and it is also an innate part of him and who he is—what he looks like, how tall he is, what he went through as a child. All these factors, and getting through some difficult childhood years because of his health, combined with his desire to do skating, which he loves so much, all brought him to his unique place in the sport."

Scott may have retired from *Stars on Ice* in 2001, but he's still on the go. "His schedule is so full, doing other things in addition to skating. He has pretty much done everything on his wish list, with the exception of one thing: doing a Broadway skating show. That gives him something to strive toward," says Sterling.

Scott's successor at the helm of *Stars on Ice* is Kurt Browning, four-time World Champion from Canada, a one-of-a-kind skater and entertainer in his own right. He has often been referred to as the Gene Kelly of the ice, because of his amazing dance ability. The continuum seems an appropriate link, as Kurt affectionately dubbed Scott "skate God for life."

"Even Kurt, when he has a bad night, it comes off with the people loving what he's done," says Dean, now a choreographer with *Stars on Ice*. "That takes a special something. If other skaters do that, the audience is like, 'Time to go off the ice now,' but with Kurt, you love him to the end."

Adds Jamie Salé, who has often said Kurt was one of her idols as she came up through the skating ranks, "Charisma like Kurt has is not something you can be taught. It's like he was born to be on the ice and perform."

"Oh boy, Kurt certainly thrives on being the center of attention. And he'll go to any extreme to get it—that's for sure," quips Brian Orser. "That can be good, and that can be bad sometimes. He's obviously one of the most well-rounded skaters that's ever been produced.

"He and I are obviously very close in terms of our development, because I retired, then he took over," Orser adds. "I watched him going through all the things I went through: the changing of the guard and having somebody right on his heels ... with Elvis Stojko, like I did with him. Sometimes it's hard—it's hard on your ego, and it's hard on your pride. But sometimes it makes you dig deep and skate even better. That's what he did for me, and I've done that for him. And Elvis made him skate better, too."

Choreographer Sandra Bezic, who first worked with Kurt as an amateur and continues to work with him in *Stars on Ice,* says there's nothing he can't do on or off the ice. "Plus, he's got this childlike spirit, which is one of the reasons why audiences love him," she adds. "He's just so accessible."

An added aspect of Kurt's skating is unpredictability. He seldom, if ever, performs a program the same way twice.

"Each time he comes out on the ice, you're excited, because you don't know what he's going to do. Kurt has been improving since the day he first skated," offers David Pelletier. "He always comes up with fantastic, entertaining programs, which is what keeps the people coming back."

Those skills stood Kurt in good stead as he created perhaps the biggest audience reaction in the three years of *Improv-ice,* performing a comedic routine to a harmonica version of the classical piece *Meditation* by Thais.

Choreographer/director Lea Ann Miller, who worked with Kurt for years in *Stars on Ice,* wishes the new generation to take note of Kurt's complete package.

"He's a natural, gifted, quick skater who is artistically brilliant. I hope more of the up-and-coming men follow in his ways on the ice. And not just do quad, quad and jump, jump. I hope that he's an example to them to learn from. He does things as a skater that you just shake your head at and wonder, *How does he do that?*" she remarks.

"When I hear a piece of music, it used to be that I would see myself skating to it. Now I see Kurt skating to it," Paul says.

"He has just an incredible fluidity and naturalness on the ice. He is able to take his personality and be this peripatetic, careless, hyperactive kid on the ice, which is really hard to do. It's really a shame that he didn't win an Olympic medal. I think that everyone is like, 'He didn't?'"

For his part, Kurt insists that good fortune has played a pivotal role in his career.

"I've always thought it had a lot to do with luck. For example, when you're in eligible skating, there can't be someone around you who is a bigger star. I always thought Christopher Bowman (former U.S. Men's Champion and two-time World medalist) was going to be the biggest star, but that never really happened. Maybe if I had skated for the U.S. and not Canada, things wouldn't have happened for me," he contends.

"You have to be lucky—lots of people are good," he adds. "They can do a quad toe, back flip, inside axel type of a move. You really have to be the right skater at the right time.

"I've always considered myself very fortunate, even though I don't have an Olympic medal. I got injured before the [1992] Olympics in Albertville and just screwed up in [1994] Lillehammer and still have what I consider a star place in figure skating. I'm just damn lucky to have that."

Hard work also has a lot to do with achieving stardom.

"I remember being at a seminar when I was 16 and having a coach tell me that I could be good, but that I wouldn't be, because I didn't work hard enough," Kurt recalls. "He sat me down, right beside my main competitor at the time, and said to me, 'You are better than him, but he will beat you every time, because he works harder than you.' I took that thought home with me."

"You need to be tough enough to be willing to practice and put in serious training," says two-time Olympic Pair Champion Ekaterina "Katia" Gordeeva. "Even if you have a great talent, if you don't support it with discipline, it can be gone."

Brian Boitano seconds that. "The work ethic is the most important thing," he offers. "I knew a lot of guys who were way more talented than me, but I think I was the first one on the ice and the last one off."

This dedication led Brian to become one of skating's few bona fide male stars. His presence on the ice is far different than the attention-driven mentalities of Kurt and Scott. Instead, Brian is a regal, powerful force, with amazing ice coverage and technical precision.

Like Scott before him and Kurt after him, Brian truly came into his element as a professional skater. He won a record six titles at the World Professional Figure Skating Championships and, in doing so, raised the bar in the professional ranks.

"In my time, it seemed like a gold medal carried a real responsibility—for representing my country and the sport," offers Brian. "I just carried that feeling over into my decision-making as a professional. For example, doing a good job on that stage. Part of this is choosing to be involved in good projects and not just do everything that is thrown your way."

You won't find a superstar in the sport that doesn't possess amazing determination.

"It's a drive that skaters have to have within themselves. You can't buy that, and your coach can't give it to you. It's either there or it's not," states Tai Babilonia. "And you can definitely tell the skaters who have it and who don't have it."

"If you're doing 100 percent all the time, it pays off," notes Elena Bechke, 1992 Olympic Pair silver medalist. "The perfect example is Paul Wylie. He always did 100 percent, if not more, which is why people love him so much.

"Paul was not necessarily that talented, and he was a short guy, but because he was so determined to please everyone watching him, that's what made him so special."

Another who has it in spades is Kristi Yamaguchi.

"Her discipline and the standards she sets are amazing. She's also the lowest maintenance skater I've ever worked with," reports Bezic.

"If I had to pick a role model for kids, I would definitely say Kristi," declares Brian Boitano. "What she's achieved in skating—her work ethic, how nice she is to people, how generous she is and how unaffected she is. Everything about Kristi is just so unassuming, just so normal. It's hard to find skaters who are that normal, but Kristi certainly is."

The business community clearly agrees with Boitano. Last year Kristi added to her list of career corporate commitments by becoming the spokesperson for SmartOnes frozen meals. In the decade since her Olympic win, Yamaguchi's corporate deals have included Celanese Acetate (which lasted 10 years), Entemanns cakes, Mervyn's California department stores and, fittingly, a promotion for platinum.

"When I work with a company, I try to give them as much of myself as I can and live up to the contract, and basically treat it in a very professional manner. That's what it deserves," states Kristi.

"Over time, you learn to balance that side of your life, the corporate side, with the skating, because they are two different things. I do think you have to be selective. You don't want all of these things pulling you away from skating, which is where you really established your identity."

A business relationship that hit close to home was her job as goodwill ambassador for the Olympic Winter Games in Salt Lake City.

"It was so special, to be a part of the Olympics in the U.S. Just being a part of what had gone on before the Olympics even started—seeing the years people put into it and how much work happened. I really was like the cheerleader for the Olympics. It was so much fun," Kristi enthuses.

Two months after the Olympics, in April, she completed a decade with the *Stars on Ice* tour. She felt that was enough—at least for now. But before she left, she got to do what she wanted most of all.

"Being able to skate pairs again, to skate with Denis (Petrov, 1992 Olympic Pair silver medalist) was such a highlight for me," shares Kristi, who won two U.S. Pair titles with Rudy Galindo before she decided to focus her energy on singles. "After nine years of doing the same thing, it's another year on tour—blah, blah, blah. It's so hard to keep reinventing yourself and doing something different and getting that same joy out of skating. Every year, I would sit and watch the pairs each night and marvel at them. I thought that was so beautiful.

"I know it's so much fun, because I've done it. I really missed it. Having that chance last season was probably my final wish in skating to be granted. It was one thing that I thought, I cannot retire without doing again."

Though her touring days may be behind her, she's still very active in skating and headlining various events. Only now she gets to enjoy spending more time at home and on the road with her husband of two years, Bret Hedican, a defenseman for the NHL's Carolina Hurricanes.

As for whether or not she will teach their future kids to skate, Kristi jokes, "If they beg, and if they say they really want to try it."

Although she thinks her husband may have the final word: "If we have boys, I think they have no choice, because Bret will have them doing hockey!"

Kristi clearly cherishes her personal life, perhaps even more so since there was a period in the mid-1990s when she had no time for one. Interest in skating had reached a fever pitch, and everyone in the business wanted a piece of her.

"It was tough. There were days where I was such a grouch. You can ask my mom. She was like, 'What's wrong with you?'" Kristi recounts. "I'd say, 'I just don't feel like I'm living my life right now. Something is holding me back, and I'm just not happy right now.'

"It was because I didn't have time for a personal life," she continues. "I consciously had to say, 'This year, before I say yes to anything, I'm going to have to sit down and think about my schedule.' Before, it was like, *It looks like a good event, I'll do it.* You can go insane, and it starts to affect the skating after a while. I just started snapping a little bit."

Despite all the acclaim and praise that has come her way over the years, Kristi still believes there is one area she can improve upon. "I always feel like I can connect even more with my audience. I feel that sometimes I don't do it enough or am doing something wrong," she laughs. "Sometimes I wish I could get people a little more into the performance."

That's an interesting assessment coming from a skater who has made it a point to explore all types of music and seems to wholeheartedly throw herself into each one.

Kristi says she is always looking back to the programs she has done and then going in the other direction. "If I haven't tried it yet, I want to go try it," she notes. "Watching Scott every night gave me the strength and confidence to do something different and have that mentality.

"His encouragement was, 'Hey, do something different, on the edge. The audience is going to get bored seeing the same thing over and over.' He kept telling me I was such a versatile skater and should explore that."

Veteran choreographer Sarah Kawahara says that's the secret to success.

"When you're working with star skaters like Scott Hamilton or Kristi Yamaguchi, it is their title that first drove them to stardom," she notes. "Then it is how they develop as professionals, and continue to develop, that keeps the audience falling in love with them. Unless the public continues to fall in love with them, then they're just looking for the next, newest, brightest star."

In the end, Kristi feels the ultimate level of success comes down to one thing. "It's integrity, really," she says. "The common bond for each skating star is that we love skating, so much so that it shows. People can grasp that and see it when we perform."

Says three-time U.S Pair Champion John Zimmerman, "If a skater is real, the audience can sense that, and you can feel them right in the palm of your hand. Or, you're in the palm of their hand. One works off the other."

Katarina Witt has captured more than her share of the crowds over the years.

Growing up in what was then East Germany, she never imagined the impact she would have on the sport and the opportunities she would have.

"I never thought I would have a professional career. So in some ways, I was very lucky for my personal life and my career that the Berlin Wall just tumbled down at the right time (1989)," she says.

"Everything started to fall in place easier for me because of this. In my amateur career, there was nothing more for me to achieve, so my dream was to become a professional," explains

Katarina.

Though she did tours such as *Holiday on Ice* and then *Skating*, which she headlined with Boitano, she didn't compete as a pro for the first few years.

"When you're an amateur skater and first look at the professional competitions, you just can't take them seriously," Katarina states. "Plus, it took a long time for me to understand that it doesn't really matter what happens at the professional competitions. It's not going to take away my reputation and what I achieved as an amateur.

"I always thought that if I get beaten, it's going to take away what I had built up as an amateur," she continues. "It took a couple years for me to understand that it doesn't. You have to be in shape, and once you are in the competition, you give your best, but it's not going to take away your crown that you earned in earlier years. People remember that you were World Champion or Olympic Champion, but they don't really remember professional competitions."

Katarina believes her diversity and willingness to adapt have served her well in terms of her popularity.

"Over the years, I've mastered the English language so much better, so I have a sense of humor in it, and people can see me on talk shows, and I always have something to talk about," she notes. "There are always new things, new projects. I think this is what has kept me interesting. Not just saying, 'Oh, she used to be an Olympic Champion.'"

On her magical connection with the audience, Katarina says, "Still, when they announce my name, I sense some mystery about it. It's like they hear my name and know, *Yeah, she's an Olympic Champion and comes from East Germany. She's been in* Playboy. *She's done this and that.*

"Hopefully, there is still some excitement and respect for what I've done and given to skating. Then they see that I live out there on the ice. I do a program and am emotionally so involved in that."

To this day, Katarina is surprised by her appeal in the U.S. "It still always amazes me how America has adopted me. A lot of times now, they don't even know that I'm from East Germany. They know I'm from Europe, and it's no big deal anymore," she says. "America honors its stars, which is nice."

Katarina has shown the current generation of women's skaters that if you play your cards right, you can be just as—if not more—powerful, sexy and admired in your 30s as in your younger days. She also feels her off-ice ventures, like *Playboy*, cameo appearances in movies such as *Ronin* and *Jerry Maguire,* and commercial ventures, enhance her on-ice appeal.

"People see there are different levels to my career," she notes. "That's why they're always interested to see 'What's she coming up with now?'"

Another of her legacies is her fierce competitiveness. "This is what separates the champion from the world-class athletes," states Katarina. "I was always able to handle it, because I knew I could do it. I was in shape. I only had to be strong enough in my head.

"First of all, you have to be physically prepared, but most of it is mental. You can't go in the competition having never done a triple axel and think all of a sudden to do a triple axel. That will never work. But if you managed to do the triple axel half of the time, you could be able to nail it, if you are mentally strong enough. That's what makes a real champion.

"I learned that I needed to be more aggressive at that moment than I was in practice. I needed to be much more forward and just go for it, don't hesitate or think twice."

Surmises Bezic, "Champions just think differently. I think most of them are probably born that way and have the ability to turn anything into a positive experience. They have the ability to stand there and believe that they can do it and have that focus and control. That attitude is really important."

While this description certainly fits Katarina to a T, with her two Olympic gold medals and four World titles, it also fits Katia Gordeeva. She has the same impressive hardware, which she earned with her late husband and partner, Sergei Grinkov.

When Sergei died of a heart attack in November 1995, the Russian Katia could have scarcely imagined the response in the U.S. The media, with its insatiable appetite for tragedy, circled its wagons around her, and made her arguably the most publicized skater for a couple years thereafter.

IMG, which represents Katia, witnessed the ensuing public sympathy for its client and quickly translated it into dollars. Katia had a national best-selling book, *My Sergei*, and was skating in TV specials from Disney's *Beauty & the Beast* to *Snowden on Ice*. She graced the cover of *People* magazine three times, donned a milk mustache for the "Got Milk" ad campaign and landed a major endorsement deal with Target stores that included her own perfume line and doll.

Reflecting back on this period, Katia feels everything was done in a tasteful manner, and she was comfortable with the projects. However, she admits, "it was a bit much," and she was relieved when the attention finally abated. "Those few years were a little hard. I was very busy and didn't have enough time to be at home with Daria (her and Sergei's young daughter). I skated a lot and did a lot of endorsements," she recalls.

While grateful for the financial security all of these opportunities brought her, Katia came to the conclusion, "I really don't want to spend all of my life doing this. It takes your time, and it takes your emotions."

While Gordeeva has scaled back her commitments on and off the ice, she still pitches Rolex watches via print ads and in the summer went on a mini-tour for Lenox Collectibles to promote the fine china figurine they created in her likeness.

So how does it feel to have your own doll, perfume and now a figurine? "Oh, I don't think about it very much," laughs Katia. "As long as it makes somebody happy, then it's good and I'm pleased with it."

This season Katia makes a resurgence in skating appearances after her reduced schedule the prior season following the birth of her daughter, Elizaveta (with Ilia Kulik, the 1998 Olympic Men's Champion).

Katia has come a long way, both professionally and personally, in the last seven years.

"She really worked her butt off after she came back to skating [in 1996], and I greatly admire her for that. For being out there, taking on singles skating, loving to perform and pushing through all the pain that I know was there," offers Paul Wylie.

Adds Rosalynn Sumners, "She's proven time and again she's not just a little waif. She's proven her strength, and she's shown us all what real strength is."

"She is an amazingly grounded person," shares Paul. "Even immediately after Sergei died. I'll never forget how she handled herself with dignity.

"I'll also never forget a comment she made to me that first season she came back to *Stars on Ice*. One night we were backstage getting ready for the finale and I was like, 'Gosh, I am really tired of doing this.' I was not excited about it and was a little uptight.

She said to me, 'Paul, life is long, but it is short. Enjoy yourself.' It really struck me. You have to relax and allow yourself to smell the roses."

That's exactly what Michelle Kwan has been doing since the post Olympic *Champions on Ice* tour ended in August.

She's opted not to compete in the eligible world's Grand Prix series of events, but is instead affording herself time to pause, reflect and ponder what direction she wants to take with her career. Is it time to turn professional or is there more left to give the eligible scene?

Michelle won't reveal her plans just yet, but says, "For the next four years, what I want from skating is just for the sport to inspire me. To have fun with it. Sometimes it's good to take things seriously, but make it alive and make it fun."

She has done just that for her many fans. Though she may not have an Olympic gold medal, it's not the deciding factor in how the public sees her. She's got a history on her side.

"You don't just come out on the scene and are a hit," offers the venerable Scott Hamilton. "You build a relationship with an audience. You build a career."

Michelle has done that. "I don't think there's an American out there who doesn't feel like they know Michelle Kwan a little bit. She's literally grown up before our eyes. That matters to people," says Kurt Browning.

Indeed, he's right. Michelle burst onto the national scene at the age of 12. By 13, she was an alternate to the Olympic team. And, unlike numerous other young prodigies, she fulfilled her promise and kept going.

At the top of the list of fast rising stars on the horizon are two new Olympic Champions: women's winner Sarah Hughes and men's victor Alexei Yagudin.

For Sarah, the final ingredients in making her feel like a star were the costumes she wore on the ice in Salt Lake City.

It may sound superfluous, but being well-dressed and looking good on the ice really matter.

"Apparently, after Nationals, there was some concern over how Sarah looked. Her coach, Robin Wagner, approached me through IMG," says costume designer Jef Billings.

"I told them I would need as much control as possible over the total package, given there was such little time before the Olympics. Not just the costume, but the hair and makeup. They were very receptive and said, 'Whatever you think is best.'

"Skaters don't skate well if they don't look good," Billings adds. "I do think I helped Sarah in some way. I know that she felt good about herself when she stepped on the ice."

Sarah agrees. "I love the dresses. They are fairy tale–like."

Since Sarah's memorable victory over Michelle Kwan and Irina Slutskaya, the offers keep pouring in.

She signed on as a spokesperson for General Electric, appeared on the cover of a Wheaties box, graced cans of Campbell's chicken noodle soup and filmed the first of two skating specials for NBC.

"I have had every opportunity I have ever wanted or imagined, and more, so there is no way I could have asked for more than that," she says.

With her commitments growing off the ice, the 17-year-old Sarah is glad she has always put such an emphasis on education, for she can now better acquit herself.

"The last years have been really crazy, but I was a very serious student. There have been a lot of times when I have placed school ahead of my skating. Right now, there are so many opportunities that, because I have been so serious about education and because

I have done so well in school, I am able to handle them much easier," Sarah reports.

"I have these skills that I didn't even realize I had developed from being such a serious student. I am able to really articulate how I feel. I am able to understand things that I wouldn't have otherwise understood, so I am glad that I spent the time that I did in school." Sarah alternates between attending public high school and tutoring, and she will graduate high school in 2003. In the autumn of 2002, she started training at a rink closer to home, so instead of a daily commute to New Jersey, she could spend more time in school.

All skating greats will tell you they didn't get to where they are by themselves. It involves surrounding yourself with the right people. And as Sumners says, "Some of those you choose, and some of them you don't."

This foundation was and is paramount for Sarah.

"She has a great family and coach. Just a great support group, and I think that's been a big part of her success," offers Michelle.

Specifically, Sarah cites her self-confidence as a big boon for her in competition. She says her parents instilled this in her and her five brothers and sisters. (Sarah is the fourth of six children ranging in ages from 11 to 25.)

"My parents have always made each of us feel like we can do anything, and so, of course, even though I knew what the reality was, I always felt like I was the greatest that I could be at that particular moment," Sarah states.

"It has been important for me to always try to take advantage of my opportunities, and if I am given something, in turn, I give a little bit more and try to work hard and expand the opportunity or do something more," she adds.

"I have always felt like I was capable of doing more, and I felt like I was a top skater even when I had only a single axel."

Robin Wagner also commends the Hughes family for the way they have allowed her to do her job as coach and choreographer.

"They have essentially entrusted me with their daughter for four years now. I always had serious conversations with Sarah's parents about what we were doing. They trusted, and they saw not only the results, but they saw how the relationship was developing, so they knew that relationship," states Wagner.

"They knew how she felt about me and how I felt about her. I think that has also helped Sarah grow as a person, by understanding loyalty, trust and sticking with it. Knowing about the people who really care about you and are looking out for you."

Sarah is quick to recognize the benefits of her connection with Wagner.

"I have been really fortunate," she says. "Not just as a student to a coach, but also to be able to spend a lot of time together traveling and going to shows—and in the car talking about things in life other than skating, such as foreign policy.

"Regarding figure skating, Robin has a great ability to look at a situation and analyze it, have an open mind and be willing to make revisions on a daily basis. It is important that I respect her decision, but she respects that I don't have to agree, because if one of us is always making rules, it is not going to work." Sarah assesses.

Skating's big question of Sarah is, will she be able to reach the same level of popularity as Michelle Kwan?

"I think it will take time. I think it is too early to tell with Sarah," reflects an honest Wagner. "I hope she maintains what she has right now. I think people love her. She is fresh. She is a new face. I think that is part of it, and I think she genuinely cares about people, and that comes through.

"When you are on that public stage, you really expose yourself. You can't help but open yourself up, and I think it is hard to sort of cheat. People see who you are, and she is a very genuine young person. She has always cared. It is just now she has the forum where she can speak out."

Some say Sarah's victory caused a huge sensation, but there wasn't enough follow through.

"I actually felt that Sarah Hughes winning was the most important thing to help skating," says Jerry Solomon, husband and manager of 1994 Olympic Women's silver medalist Nancy Kerrigan. "The disappointing thing is that I don't see her gold medal having the whip-like effect that I thought it was going to. I don't even know what she's doing right now. You don't see her, hear of her. She's sort of disappeared.

"It's unfortunate that [the way she and her family have handled things] aren't in concert with what's in the best interest of the sport," he adds. "To some degree right now, it is, as Sarah Hughes goes, so goes the sport. So if she's going to take [the moderate] kind of approach, which may be the right thing to do for her, for the totality of her life, the sport has to be on a different timetable."

For Sarah, winning the Olympics is the beginning, not a final note.

"She looks at being the Olympic Champion not as merely a stepping stone to get to other places," offers Wagner. "She takes it as a serious responsibility and wants to use the title to reach out to other people and help them."

On the ice, Sarah, who has her sights set on winning her first U.S. and World titles this year, has no intention of leaving the eligible world anytime soon.

"The Olympics was like a dream competition for me. It was so magical," she says. "I want to keep expanding as a person and as a skater, and if I can do that, I would love to take part in another Olympics."

That's also in the back of Alexei Yagudin's mind, ever the intense competitor.

"I would like to keep myself in a good shape, because it was so hard to get in this shape and to get used to that, so I don't want to lose it right away. And I feel that I can accomplish more in the sport," explains Alexei.

"I'm not sure about the next Olympics. It might happen, but I realize that if I will quit, or do little competing for one or two years, the odds are against me going back. But that's what people are basically saying to me, 'Take two years off and come back.' But as an athlete, I just know that there's no way to do that."

This season, however, he has focused his attention on doing the *Stars on Ice* tour and may or may not be at the World Championships to defend his title.

What is certain is that skating experts believe Alexei will be the first Russian male skater to become a superstar.

Offers Kurt, "Alexei will have to work really, really hard to make himself endearing to the American public—it's not just going to happen naturally for him. But, I think he's the right guy to do it. He has all the ingredients."

Sterling says the key to Alexei capturing the American audience comes down to one thing. "He speaks good English now, but he needs to speak *really* good English," Sterling says. "That's the main factor to really cross over with the public and for marketing and endorsement purposes."

Meanwhile, Alexei, who has lived in the U.S. for four years, believes his emotions and personality will lead him to fame.

"The main thing is to be able to open up and show yourself to people. To be able to take someone's heart, then that is what makes you a star," he says.

So what does Alexei wish for his skating future? "I want to do the same thing Kristi Yamaguchi and Brian Orser did. They have been involved in skating for so many years, and they won a lot, but they act like innocents. They are honest, and they are such good people. They are idols for me," Alexei shares.

"I want to be involved in figure skating as long as I can. Be on *Stars on Ice* for many years, keep competing and just bring happiness to people."

It is Alexei's warm persona, which lends itself to grabbing hold of an audience, that sets him apart from some other past Russian champions. Plus, he has a drive and a belief that he can make it big, a notion shared by his management company, IMG, which is pushing him front and center at every turn. It cannot be underestimated how, in skating, like the real world, connections and support like this can make or break you.

For it is a sports agent that is behind the deals to participate in skating events and deals with corporate America for commercial endorsements, as well as overall promotion, media interviews and appearances. An agent can wear any number of hats, from that of advisor, to negotiator, to salesman—and even baby sitter.

"An agent can be involved in almost every aspect for a skater," says Rosenberg. "That can translate into more than just getting and sustaining work. From personal lives, to green cards, to weddings and more."

Ilia Kulik, Alexei's countryman and Olympic predecessor, says he never thought about breaking into the top tier of skating celebrities, because that's normally reserved only for North Americans.

"It wasn't an issue for me. It wasn't a problem. I didn't come in here thinking I would be a huge, huge star," Ilia contends. "I wasn't expecting standing ovations every night. I'm happy every time I see people interested in my skating. That is what motivates me to keep going. If I see people liking it, people excited about it, I'm already really happy with it."

Offers Sterling, "Ilia's years with *Stars on Ice* were phenomenal. Coming out of the Olympics, he was one of *People*'s 50 Most Beautiful. There was extreme excitement and energy there, but he was not the showman that he became this past season.

"Ilia brought to *Stars on Ice* some extraordinary things with his choreography and with the numbers he was doing. He could do the classical stuff. He could do this amazing hip stuff. That is exciting to see."

With his gold medal and good looks—not to mention his great grasp of the English language, it looked like Ilia could be the guy to take figure skating by storm.

And while he's had a good career to date, it's not translated to superstar status. So what happened?

He spent the last four years with the IMG-produced *Stars on Ice* tour, but never became an IMG client. That definitely didn't help matters, since IMG is the hub of most skating work and promotion.

Instead, he enlisted the help of the show biz–focused William Morris Agency. This relationship did lead to an opportunity outside of the sport, when he was cast in a supporting role in the 2000 feature film *Center Stage*. It was a nice debut for an acting novice, but he hasn't followed up on that, he says, due to his skating demands.

Sterling says it all boils down to personality and desire. "Ilia doesn't skate or do whatever as a matter of proving anything to anybody," he says. "It's for self-satisfaction.

"With Ilia and with Katia (Gordeeva, his mate) as well, you are looking at two people who are really very private and very true to their Russian heritage. They have come here because it is a better life in this country, and they were rewarded for their efforts."

"Ilia loves what America has given to him, but when it comes to really getting on the bandwagon, that is not the place he or Katia want to be."

One example would be publicity. When Katia gave birth to their daughter, Liza, in 2001, *People* magazine stood ready to publish a feature story. Ilia only grudgingly allowed a small mention on *People*'s Passages page and no photo. He still declines to answer any personal questions, and news of the duo's presumed marriage in 2002 remains clouded in secrecy.

"I'm trying to keep my private life for myself," he explains. "I'm a person who can enjoy it more when it's private. In America, it's so different. In Russia, people care more what you do as a performer. It's a different mentality.

"For me, it's really hard to switch," he adds. "I don't know if I'll ever adjust to this."

In stark contrast, however, is a very Americanized Alexei, who openly talks about one day seeking U.S. citizenship and is willing to play the games necessary to make it big with the media and general public.

As a rule, who has a more difficult time becoming a skating star than a Russian man?

Try a pair team.

But when Canada's Jamie Salé & David Pelletier brought fans at the Delta Center in Salt Lake City to their feet, that all seemed to change.

They were the stars of the 2002 Winter Games.

The duo, who most thought should have won the pair gold medal on the night of the free skate, but who wound up with a gold medal at the end of the week, has since had an interesting journey.

Pure and simple, their then-agent Craig Fenech, who had never represented skaters before, overestimated their market value. Apart from Crest Whitestripes, they were unable in the U.S. to cash in on being the most talked about story from the Olympics. Not only that, their asking price squeezed them out of any post-Olympic tours, keeping them out of the limelight. But that was only after what was supposed to be their own tour failed to materialize.

"They got a tremendous amount of publicity. They skated extremely well. There was a tremendous controversy about the gold medal. I really feel they're not getting a fair shake in certain areas of the business. It's just bad management," declares Tom Collins.

The ill-fated Salé and Pelletier tour was to feature fellow 2002 Olympic Pair Champs Elena Berezhnaya & Anton Sikharulidze, plus Brian Boitano and Oksana Baiul.

It didn't happen, because you simply can't put together a tour that quickly, says Collins.

"You have to get dates in buildings where you can play. You've got *Stars on Ice* out there. We're out there with *Champions on Ice*. They were thinking of doing this tour right in the middle of our schedule," he says.

Most specifically, *Stars on Ice* and *Champions on Ice* have exclusive contracts with arenas, which stipulate that similar ice shows are barred from playing there within a certain time frame of their standing dates.

In 2001, shortly after Jamie and David had signed with him, Fenech candidly told *International Figure Skating* he knew little about the sport, but it looked like it would be an interesting challenge.

"Really, what it's about is understanding the context more than anything else," Fenech said. "If you know how to negotiate, you know how to negotiate.

"People laugh when I tell them I'm doing skating," he added. "Because they think, *You've been doing baseball, football, that kind of thing*. I said, 'The hair was standing up on my arms watching (at the 2001 Worlds in Vancouver).' It was thrilling."

But thrilling, and even a genuine enthusiasm, don't get you a job. Jamie and David eventually took on a new manager and promptly signed to tour with both the U.S. and Canadian versions of *Stars on Ice*. Their first performance after the signing was the closing show of *Skate the Nation*, IMG's tour through the smaller Canadian arenas, in Saskatoon, Saskatchewan.

Prior to that, Kurt echoed the sentiments of skating community, "I hope they don't end up regretting what they're doing. I'm surprised and confused," he said.

It was not a pleasant experience, reflects Jamie. "We just had an unfortunate time," she reports. "We were led in a direction that we did not want to be led in. We know our reputation isn't ruined … but we did miss being on tour this summer."[1]

Offers David, "What we went through, no one really knows. In this situation, we lost control. Now we're taking it back."[2]

While the buzz was that Jamie and David had fired Fenech, he says he resigned. He gave several interviews saying how the golden duo had allowed others to undermine him, and he couldn't function effectively. But he does acknowledge they didn't try to persuade him to remain on.

A couple both on and off the ice, they choose not to dwell on possible missteps. "I think people who regret have really unsatisfied careers or unsatisfied lives. I've been over-satisfied with what I've done," David remarks. "I never thought I was going to make it this far. We never look back. We always look forward."

Which, considering everything, is a good outlook for them.

"They could have done very, very well, but now it's too late. The Olympics are a very short-lived thing. After six months, if a skater or skaters don't promote themselves, it's very difficult. I don't think they can ever recoup what might have been,"[3] assesses Collins.

Believes Brian Boitano, "With an Olympic gold medal, you have a built-in great image right off the bat, but how well known you are and become is really based on what you do afterwards."

The public's memory can indeed be short and its taste fickle.

To keep the attention, it often pays to have an individual place in the sport.

Scott Hamilton is the caring cutup.

Kurt Browning is the charismatic dancer.

Brian Boitano is the majestic presence.

Katarina Witt is the sex symbol.

Katia Gordeeva is the steel magnolia.

And Elvis Stojko is the rebel warrior. The two-time Olympic Men's silver medalist and three-time World Champion from Canada has battled back from injury time and again—and always bucked the trend in favor of his unique, brash style.

Following the beat of his own drum has cost him. The reserved judges wouldn't give him the title at the 1994 Winter Games. Yet it is his style that has set him apart with fans.

Elvis says he decided early on in his skating career that he was going to do what he believed in, no matter what.

"Sure, at times it was frustrating. It wasn't easy. But I wanted to keep pushing forward and not change the way I am about my skating and try to be something that I am not," he explains. "I love techno, hip-hop and rock 'n' roll. That's my style. But I would constantly hear, 'Oh, he doesn't have style.'"

Elvis faced this sentiment from those at home and elsewhere.

"This came from judges from my own country, judges from other countries and, in general, the hierarchy in skating," he reports.

But others gave him support, albeit not publicly. "There were people who would come by very quietly and would not want anybody to really hear. They would say, 'You know what, I love what you are doing. Stick to it,'" Elvis recalls.

"I am not one to follow the masses, and I hope no one is pressured to follow my path, because I want them to go out on their own. I could never skate like Brian [Orser] or Kurt [Browning]. I followed my heart.

"The audience isn't stupid," he continues. "They know if you are being fake. They know if you are out there doing your thing and enjoying it and if you are yourself. That is what I have always done. I felt that I could be myself and be able to take my skating to another level."

Genuine is almost a buzzword in skating—coming up time and again from Katarina, Kristi and Tara Lipinski.

"Whatever I do, it's really genuine," says Tara.

"The public can feel it," echoes Oksana Baiul. "You cannot fool them."

From individualism, to hard work, to a powerful sports agent, to an engaging personality. These ingredients, and many more, go into the making of a modern skating star. It's a recipe the established icons have followed for years.

"Stardom is really a personal challenge more than anything else. It's a love/hate thing. It's like a writer—what's their next book? It's a continual process of topping oneself," says Christopher Dean. "You need to be up to the task."

Believes Katarina, "People remember a skater's name, plus something they were emotionally moved by—a story or a program. Those are the stars who have given back to skating by being idols, by being role models and trying to keep going, giving their experiences to the sport. And for that, we are rewarded."

[1, 2, 3] Amy Rosewater, *The New York Times*, July 23, 2002

Lights, Camera—Public

"In the U.S., people try to know more than they need to know, beyond the skating to the personal life. I'm not sure if it's good or bad. Because if they know you better, it probably brings more people and more interest to you as a skater."

– Ilia Kulik,
1998 Olympic Men's Champion

Lights, Camera—Public

R ecognition doesn't come with an on/off switch. Whether at center ice in a packed arena or at the checkout of a 7-Eleven, skaters quickly learn that any time can be "show time."

Some skaters choose to embrace the adulation, while others proceed more cautiously.

For Ekaterina "Katia" Gordeeva, becoming comfortable with her celebrity and all of its trappings wasn't immediate or natural, largely because American culture is so different than that of her homeland. "The newspapers and press talk much more about celebrities in the U.S. than in Russia. They're more interested to get inside the private lives. In Russia, yes, you do several interviews and yes, maybe you are on TV, but it's more about your work, your achievements," she explains.

Katia got a crash course in the U.S. media and public admiration after her husband and skating partner Sergei Grinkov died suddenly in 1995. When she penned the touching *My Sergei* memoir the following year, she didn't quite realize the floodgates of curiosity it would open. "It has bothered me," Katia admits. "People read the book and know about my life already, so then they want to continue to know me and what's happening in my personal life."

The interest intensified in 1999 when she began a romantic relationship with Ilia Kulik. (The couple welcomed a daughter, Elizaveta, in June 2001.)

"At times it's been a little hard, but I didn't go very crazy because I've always had a supportive family and had somewhere I could go. It wasn't like, *Oh, my God, I spent all of my life there, all of myself with the public*," states Katia.

To a large extent, she has now come to terms with her fame. "That's what it's all about in the United States. People want to know what's happening in celebrities' lives. Sometimes though, you want privacy, so you have to take time out from the public life and have it be only for your family. That's very important."

For his part, Ilia says he's "totally fine" with spending time with fans and enjoys that connection. But he is adamant that his and Katia's personal life is off-limits, both for fans and for the media.

At his first pro victory in December 2001 at the Hallmark Skaters' Championship, a reporter at the press conference simply asked how his new baby was doing. Ilia replied, "No personal questions."

He insists, "The main focus has to be the things I'm doing on the ice. My belief is skating—that's where the knowing starts and where it's got to finish."

Michelle Kwan agrees.

"There have to be limitations. Sometimes I feel people don't recognize them," she states. "I understand people are curious. Of course I want to be open and tell the truth, but when it comes to my personal life and not skating, that's a little different.

"I feel bad for celebrities like (actress/singer) Jennifer Lopez. Her relationships are all over the magazines. And suddenly, eight months later, something happens to the relationship and the public is talking. I don't want any part of that," says Michelle.

"Overall, I've always been very open in interviews with the media and with the public. I don't hide too much. Maybe I'm a little too forthcoming," she wonders.

That's seldom the case with Brian Boitano.

"I've always been really, really private. I try to keep everybody sort of at arm's length without offending them too much," he admits. "If you let people get too familiar it can be a problem, and I've had those problems before.

"It's something that every skater needs to address and decide how important it is in his or her life to keep the separation. Some skaters might like that attention," Brian surmises.

Kurt Browning, for one, does.

"As for people wanting to know about me, I've always been able to justify it with the fact that they love skating as much as I do; they just don't skate. I've always enjoyed people, enjoyed the fans," shares Kurt.

"I've always been told, though, that I let too many people in my personal space. But you know what? Generally speaking, it doesn't take that much time, and it's fun. Then one day it's gone, so why not take pleasure in it!"

Kurt's talent, effervescence and rapport with people have afforded him some of skating's most loyal fans—many of whom travel to virtually all of his performances. While appreciative, he questions that some don't have their priorities straight. "There are always a few out there that you kind of look at in the eye and go, 'You really should go home and spend more time with your husband. You've spent so much money to go to so many shows,'" he declares.

"I can say that because I've seen them so many times I'm starting to get a glimpse into their lives. And that's the only time it's ever bothered me ... when I see people that I think are sometimes putting skating so high up on the level of things to do. I want to say, 'Are you sure this is the right thing for you?'"

Like Kurt, Tara Lipinski loves her public life and meeting fans. She has an official Web site that she frequently visits where fans can chat and leave messages for her. "I love to read what my fans say. I find that they are so supportive of me. It's wonderful," she enthuses.

Tara, however, has also experienced the flip side of the "plugged-in" generation.

Skating message boards abound on the Internet, some of which are devoted solely to slamming particular skaters. Tara is at the top of the list—and she knows it!

"Those sites make me feel really depressed. I simply avoid them. I know the ones that are bad, and I just don't go there," she says.

Her new *Stars on Ice* castmates Jamie Salé & David Pelletier were thrust into a worldwide media spotlight amidst the pairs judging controversy at the 2002 Winter Olympics in Salt Lake City.

The couple became overnight stars and appeared on the *Today Show*, the *Tonight Show* and the covers of *Time* and *Newsweek*. Dealing with such fame has proven to take a bit of adjustment.

"It's very weird for us. Dave and I are very surprised all the time when people come up to us and catch us off guard," says Jamie. "We think we're invisible and we hear, 'Hey, there's the Canadian skaters.' It's weird in a funny way, in a good way. It's not like we don't like it."

"We do get recognized, although when I'm by myself I get a little lucky and maybe nobody knows me," laughs David. "When I'm with Jamie, we get recognized a lot. When I'm by myself, it's about 50 percent less.

"We've gone to celebrity golf tournaments, and we're there with the big stars and you don't think people will know you, but obviously a lot of people watched the Olympics. Plus our faces were in the papers so many times. It's fun and you do the best with it. People are nice and it's cool," he says.

The duo enjoyed such an amazing public response that they had to hire someone to organize all of their fan mail. "We're getting hundreds and hundreds of pieces of mail a week. Also, we have a lot of people going on our Web site. It's pretty overwhelming," admits Jamie. "It's important to us though, so we take time out of our day to sign 500 or however many post cards are being mailed."

The way the public took Jamie and David under its wing was reminiscent of what happened at the 1980 Lake Placid Olympics with American pair skaters Tai Babilonia & Randy Gardner, who were one of the favorites for the pair gold medal, but who had to withdraw due to Randy's groin injury.

"I came home to so much fan mail. It was incredible. People would send articles and clippings and I was like, 'Oh my God, we really affected some people here,'" recalls Tai.

"What Jamie and David went through was like 100 times more. I can't even imagine. Skating is so popular today, whereas when it happened to us, the sport had just started to resonate with people."

When skating reached its peak of popularity a few years ago, nobody was harder at work or spread as thin as Kristi Yamaguchi, who readily admits she felt the strain of her public demands.

"I felt I was living three lives: a small, little life with Bret (Hedican, then boyfriend and now husband), my skating life and my public life. My public life was even taking away from my skating and frustrating me. I couldn't even train five days a week, because I was making all of these appearances," says Kristi.

Newly crowned Olympic champ Alexei Yagudin can sympathize. "Sometimes there's so much to do and you really hate to do it, but other times you really like to get to know new people," he shares. "Sometimes you are really tired, but I know that's another part of my job that I have to do."

Alexei says he's not often recognized in the U.S. and can stroll pretty much unnoticed on the streets of New York City. But in Canada, it's a different story.

"I think the Canadians are the best. They really don't care who you are or where you're from. They just love skating," he describes. "The American people like their own skaters more. You can be a several-times World Champion or twice Olympic Champion from another country, then only if you skate well will the Americans kind of come in closer and warm to you."

"I've got more titles than everyone in *Champions on Ice*, but still I did not get that response from the audience, because I'm not an American," he says.

That same sentiment can be applied to the press as well, says Lynn Plage, publicity director for the *Champions on Ice* tour.

"The Russians are very cooperative in wanting to do interviews, but the hard part is convincing a reporter they are as important as the Americans," she says. "I tell the press it's not just the Russians trying to beat the Americans. They all get along when they're on tour; they have fun together. So why don't you give it a try and talk to them?"

Alexei is certainly willing to shoot the breeze. The day after he won the men's title at the 2002 European Championships, he held an impromptu press conference all by his lonesome, because he was tired the night before during the scheduled one. He felt he had more to say and knew the audience there would be a captive one. The press conference lasted well over an hour.

Alexei clearly thrives on connecting with people, and he is grateful for all of his fans. "Without them, it would be hard for me to make money and earn a living," he notes. "The fans help us skaters, and of course it's good to know that there are so many people behind you and supporting you."

Up-and-comer Jennifer Kirk, a member of the 2002 U.S. World Team, appears to already have a firm handle on the public side of her sport.

"It's really important to keep in mind that once you reach a certain level that people start watching you. You need to realize, when they cheer for you, they want to cheer for you as a person, not just your skating," says the 18-year-old. "I try to do the right thing and be nice to people and care about the people who are talking to me."

Whether building a public persona or maintaining an established celebrity, skaters are expected to be on call for the press after they skate in a competition, while on tour and via the telephone from the rink or even home.

It comes with the territory, but it isn't always a walk in the park.

"It's hard, because you compete and the media wants to interview you right after you get your marks. Sometimes you skate badly and go around the corner and see all these reporters asking you questions, but you can't show that you're really upset. You can't think about it, you just go on automatic. You have to keep cool," says Jennifer.

"Skating is such a subjective sport that you need to realize, if you handle yourself improperly, sometimes it can hurt your skating. You have to always be on your best behavior."

Then there are the competition press conferences, where occasionally sparks fly.

"The media is always trying to get people to fight in those," contends 2002 Olympic Ice Dance Champion Gwendal Peizerat. "The media always asks something like, 'Do you consider yourself better than the other teams?' Or, 'What makes you better than so and so?' This stuff happens all the time."

Last year, Michelle Kwan was at the center of one of the most unforgettable press conferences in recent memory. The setting was following the women's event at the 2001 Skate America competition, where Michelle beat Sarah Hughes in a somewhat controversial decision.

Several prominent members of the media verbally pounced on Michelle and point-blank told her she did not deserve the victory. Michelle kept her cool during the barrage, but was noticeably shaken afterwards. Her agent, Shep Goldberg, was fuming and running around demanding answers and apologies.

"My mouth dropped open because that was the rudest thing I've heard in my life," recalls Michelle. "And the media expected me to answer their attack. What gives them the power to treat people like that?"

Win or lose an event, Michelle has learned firsthand that there's no escaping the media's intense glare. "There were a few years that I didn't understand why they asked me certain questions. At times, I felt they were mean. I'm a human being. I make mistakes and don't succeed all of the time," she states. "You can feel so intruded upon and so violated, but you just have to put it in perspective.

"I've gotten used to it now, though," she adds. "It's gotten to the point that what the media says and what the media asks me doesn't really even register with me. Luckily, I have my parents, family and friends to help me. I can only imagine what it's like if you don't have a support system, because you can just get pounded on by these people."

Reigning Olympic Women's Champion Sarah Hughes was thankful she had her family and coach Robin Wagner around her for the media onslaught leading up to the Salt Lake City Games, because the demands were pulling her in many different directions.

"It was incredibly wearing, because now I wasn't getting tired because of working on the ice or getting physically exhausted, I was getting exhausted from going to appearances and interviews and photo shoots," Sarah declares. "Everybody wants a piece of you ... and it was so odd to me and so foreign, because I didn't even skate yet. I wasn't even at the Olympics. Everybody just wants something to show before the Olympics, and it's just a lot of hype."

Hughes obviously was able to walk this tightrope, but only after feeling she had been thrown to the media wolves a few months earlier, when she won the Skate Canada Grand Prix event over both Michelle Kwan and Irina Slutskaya.

"I was constantly asked, 'How did it feel to win?' 'How did it feel to beat so-and-so?' And I really didn't like the questions," she says. "I was tired from the first two competitions, and I got a little off track. I knew a lot of people then questioned me and said, 'She is faltering. She has got a little spotlight and look what happens.

She wasn't ready to handle it.'

"It was pretty shallow, I thought. It wasn't even a couple of weeks after I won, but then people started considering me as a contender. It didn't change my view of myself. It changed everybody else's view of me."

Jamie Salé & David Pelletier can relate to the pre-Olympic pressure, which reached a fever pitch in their native Canada.

"We were bombarded with people asking us how you could move (from Montreal to Edmonton) in an Olympic year and leave our coach, blah, blah, blah. You know what, we realized it was going to get worse from there and just prepared ourselves for it," says Jamie.

"We said to everybody that we're not doing any more interviews after a certain date," she continues. "It was really hard to stick to that, because we didn't want to get a bad reputation or have bad quotes in the paper, but they had to understand that we had to train. We couldn't be distracted. Most people respected that pretty well."

"We came to embrace it. We would be foolish to say the attention and pressure came as a surprise to us," remarks David. "We knew it was going to be like this, because of how it was at the [2001] World Championships in Vancouver. That was a great warm up for that, having the Worlds in your own country and in Canada—North America. So we sort of knew what to expect from the media leading up to our event. After it was over, that was another story."

The pressure the Canadian public unwittingly put on Jamie and David was even harder to deal with.

"When you were going to buy something at the store, people would say, 'Good luck at the Olympics. Don't come back without the gold medal. We'll be cheering for you,'" Jamie recalls. "You sleep it, you live it the few days of competition at the Olympics. So to have to talk about it is too much. I have to say that the last six months leading up to it were the absolute worst. I'm not going to cover that up at all. It was awful. Dave and I were so on edge every day.

"We were trying to have fun, but it was a miserable time, too, because you are so stressed. You want everything to be so perfect. And then people are always saying things to you like, 'Are you excited? When do you leave?' It's like, *Oh my God!* You've got to get away from it, because you can't talk about it all the time; that's not healthy. So we took it day by day, and we had each other."

Of all the skaters, it is perhaps Nancy Kerrigan who has endured the toughest times in the public eye. She was put through the wringer by the media following her attack at the 1994 U.S. Nationals and hounded virtually everywhere she went leading up to the Lillehammer Olympics and immediately thereafter.

If anyone in skating has earned the right to offer a few words of retort to the press, it is Nancy.

"The media needs to treat skaters with respect. The same respect they would wish upon themselves or their parents. Just be courteous and thoughtful because we have feelings," she says.

"They don't know what the future holds either. Somebody that's going to say something bad about me then, in five or 10 years might want something from me. You never know."

The Studios

"We were clearly first and the leader in the professional skating world, then it got very competitive once everybody saw that it was going well. Everybody jumped on and tried to compete with us and started doing competitions. Now most all of them have gone away, because it's not quite so easy anymore. We're in it for the long haul. We're committed to skating."

– Bob Kain, President and COO, Americas,
International Management Group

The Studios

As in the Hollywood of yesteryear, when the studios controlled everything and everybody involved with the silver screen, so, too, is today's figure skating.

Comparable to Metro-Goldwyn-Mayer and Warner Brothers, skating has Tom Collins Enterprises and IMG.

They rule every aspect of high profile skating. The talent. The buildings. The sponsors. The television networks. The coveted jobs.

If you have dreams of stardom, they are the only two games in town.

Inclusion in either of these skating studios is a clear sign you are somebody in skating. You've been accepted, and, most importantly, you've probably got a nice paycheck.

Tom Collins Enterprises, which produces the *Champions on*

Ice tours, is owned by Tom Collins, who is the epitome of a rags-to-riches tale. His humble beginnings as the son of a gold miner in a small town in Ontario, Canada, led to sitting on a gold mine in later years. Collins' fierce determination to succeed is evident in the way he does business with his skaters. Like Louis B. Mayer in film's golden era, you're either Collins' friend or you're not. End of story.

Then there is the billion-dollar IMG, a sports marketing behemoth, which has interests in every major sport and is one of the largest producers of television. Its figure skating interests are governed by Bob Kain, President and COO, Americas, IMG, who oversees *Stars on Ice* in the U.S. and Canada, manages the production of numerous skating events and has sponsorship contracts with the International Skating Union (ISU) that alone are valued at over $80 million. Running Winter Sports in IMG's New York office is Jay Ogden, a corporate attorney with a buttoned-down style.

Tom Collins' first major entrée into figure skating was as a show skater with *Holiday on Ice* in the 1950s and 1960s. During his 22-year tenure with the show, he climbed the ladder to become a principal performer. He had the honor of working with the legendary Sonja Henie and even had a private audience with the pope in Rome.

The owner of *Holiday on Ice* took Collins under his wing and taught him the business—such as how arenas are run, how to book shows and how to move shows in and out. Collins also learned the ropes by working as a promoter for the premier skating show of its time, *Ice Capades*.

Collins started his own tour, which ran after the World Championships, in 1969. It was far from the spectacular display it is today and has gone through several name incarnations.

"We used to travel around with two black fiber suitcases. I'd have in there the banner that went around the hockey boards and a small tape recorder. That was it," recalled Collins in a 1997 interview with *International Figure Skating* magazine. "We would come in. The skaters would put up the banner around the ice. We'd hook our tape machine up to the building sound, and that was our equipment until 1988.

"Then we made major changes to sounds and lights. But through 1987, that's the way we traveled. A lot of people don't know that. They think it was always this big production from its inception."

The change in scale for the tour, then called *Tour of World Figure Skating Champions*, coincided with the 1988 Olympics in North America—in Calgary, Alberta, Canada.

Brian Boitano, once the tour mainstay, remembers what it was like that year and how the crowds really started embracing skating.

"It was wild and really cool," Boitano says. "It was like a rock show, and we were rock stars. Then, people weren't used to seeing so much skating, and when you came out and did those tours, the people were so excited and wanted to see you so badly."

The 1988 tour also marked when the tour went to an annual basis. In the 1970s, it had primarily occurred every two to three years. It became more frequent in the 1980s, but still did not occur annually.

In 1989, professionals were able to join the cast. In 1996, Collins debuted the winter tour. Two years later, in 1998, he changed the show's name to *Champions on Ice*.

The tours are sanctioned by the United States Figure Skating Association (USFSA), Skate Canada (the skating governing body in Canada) and the International Skating Union (ISU), so Collins can hire both Olympic-eligible and professional skaters. It's a win-

win formula. (Due to the scheduling of the winter tour, which occurs at the height of the eligible competitive season, only professional skaters are generally on board.)

Collins runs his ice troupe like any studio chief would. He controls every aspect of his show, including approval of skaters' music and programs. While he gives the heavy-hitters more of a free rein, he's not shy about letting people know what works best for them, and from time to time, he's insisted a skater do a certain number.

Do you really think that five years after its debut, Rudy Galindo still wants to be skating to The Village People medley? It was the boss' idea.

Collins even directed one skater, who wanted to go back to her roots, to continue bleaching her hair blonde for the tour. "He said that's how people recognize me," she says.

When it comes to the business aspect with his skaters, Collins can be even more unyielding.

He has been known to strong-arm skaters with exclusive, long-term contracts. Todd Eldredge, for one, likely won't be sending him a Christmas card! When Eldredge attempted to jump ship in 1999 during his multi-year contract, Collins let him know that wasn't going to happen. Often, the skaters must first receive his blessing to skate in another promoter's event that may be playing in one of "his" buildings—where he has a deal for his own show.

Reigning Olympic Pair co-gold medalists Elena Berezhnaya & Anton Sikharulidze have felt Collins' wrath.

According to Berezhnaya and Sikharulidze's coach, Tamara Moskvina, in February, when Collins got wind that the Russians were going to join rival tour *Stars on Ice* in the fall, after their *Champions on Ice* contract was up, he promptly decided there was no room for them on the post-Olympic tour.

"Elena and Anton really planned all along on doing this tour. However, Tom Collins simply did not invite them to participate," states Moskvina.

Collins, however, says otherwise. He says he did offer the Russian pair a spot in the show. They declined, in favor of participating in a "Golden Pairs" tour (which never materialized) being organized by Craig Fenech, then-manager of fellow co-gold medalists Jamie Salé & David Pelletier, and sports entrepreneur Mike Burg.

In 1999, Alexei Yagudin, then the reigning World Men's Champion (now also the Olympic Champion), was booted from the tour in midstream for bad behavior. In 2000, he spent the spring and early summer relaxing, and in 2001, he performed with *Stars on Ice* Canada. He only rejoined *Champions on Ice* in 2002, for the post-Olympic run. To this day, Alexei is not 100 percent sure why he was so suddenly dismissed.

Prior to his return to the show, he questioned both Tom Collins and his son, Michael, the tour manager. "I asked them, 'Can you please explain to me why I was out the last time?' Michael apologized. But I still feel it wasn't right, what they did to me before."

Yagudin contends his ousting perhaps had something to do with his former coach, Alexei Mishin, who had originally struck his deal with Collins, only to see his skater leave him for another coach. No loyalty was shown by Yagudin towards his coach; no loyalty was shown to Yagudin by Collins.

Regardless, Yagudin made sure to be careful and mind his Ps and Qs on his 2002 stint—keeping largely to himself. He joins the U.S. *Stars on Ice* tour this season. He says he's learned the hard way that there's a big difference between the environment in *Champions on Ice* and *Stars on Ice*.

"I know that on *Stars* everybody cares about you, so if something bad happens, they will cover that. They will hide it, and it will never go public," he asserts. "If something happens or never happens, but is just said to happen on *Champions*, nobody cares, because they have so many first, second and third place champions that you're not that important."

Yet others, like Michelle Kwan, who annually headlines Collins' spring/summer program, display loyalty that knows no bounds.

"It is different to any other tour," says Michelle, who has been offered a spot in *Stars on Ice* several times. "It is because Tom Collins is so special, because he takes it personally. I like a family owned business, and it's run that way. It is like McDonald's vs. Joey's Café. It's got a relaxed atmosphere, and that makes it fun. It is important for us, because we can mix business and pleasure together, and it is like the best of both worlds."

It's not only Michelle who has not wavered in devotion. Over the last decade, neither have Viktor Petrenko, Nancy Kerrigan, Oksana Baiul and Isabelle Brasseur & Lloyd Eisler.

Michael Rosenberg, well-known skating agent and long-time friend of Collins, says the reason is cut-and-dried—the skaters are treated wonderfully.

"Tommy rides in the bus with them and doesn't ride in a limo. He eats with them and sits and listens to their personal problems. And if he can, he helps them with personal problems. The door is always open to his office. He is so open to talk to, to laugh with, to have dinner with and to become personally involved with," Rosenberg offers.

"The skaters have such a great loyalty to him, because they're treated like they are family, not like they are contracted employees. If you're treated that way—and obviously his tour is first class—you want to stay."

Collins has been known to lavish expensive gifts on skaters who have been with the tour for a long period of time. Skaters who reach a 10-year mark with the tour receive gold Rolex watches. Once, he gifted Brian Boitano with a car. He is also known in the skating world as a gracious host. Each year at the U.S. National Championships, he throws a huge party attended by all the glitterati. At Worlds, he hosts private dinner parties at the most exclusive restaurants in town.

His generosity doesn't end with the skaters and is not given without expecting loyalty in return, contends Oksana Baiul's former agent, Michael Carlisle.

"The game that Tommy has played—and that has helped him survive for so many years competing with IMG so well—is that he took care of the coaches and [countries'] federation leaders," reveals Carlisle.

"For example, Valetin Piseev (president of the Figure Skating Federation of Russia) would come to Florida or California as Tommy's guest. Galina (Zmievskaya, Baiul's former coach) was a recipient as well. If not money, certainly attention, so that Oksana would skate for Tommy and not go to IMG."

In a brief interview in the spring of 2002, Collins said such considerations have been a two-way street. "I've been very, very good to the skaters, and they have been very, very good to me. They know it, and I know it. I never had any doubts about certain ones leaving me to go somewhere else to work. I would have been shocked if it would have happened. I just never, ever thought about it," he said.

But what about those skaters who haven't stayed? The ones who went on to *Stars on Ice*: Todd, Elena and Anton, Ilia Kulik and Tara Lipinski, to name a few.

"Those who didn't have a great loyalty to him and a great feeling of positive energy toward Tommy would be ungrateful and spoiled," charges Rosenberg. "And those are the kind of people who have no loyalty and will always change and never blame themselves for their problems. They change agents, they change coaches, they change choreographers and they change tours. It's never them."

In fact, several people close to the tour say Collins was particularly hurt by Kulik.

Beyond the loyalty, beyond the perks, there is another reason most North American skaters stay with Collins for the duration of their eligible skating careers.

Unlike for *Champions on Ice*, the USFSA does not provide a blanket sanction for *Stars on Ice*. However, the USFSA can make individual exceptions for skaters as it sees fit. Skate Canada only sanctions the brief Canadian leg of *Stars on Ice*.

The translation is that if you're North American and want to tour in the U.S. and be assured of retaining your eligibility to compete in events such as Nationals and Worlds, *Champions on Ice* is the only sure bet.

The reason for Collins to have such an arrangement is quite simple. He wants the sport's brightest North American eligible stars—the ones who bring fans to the arena—on his tour. Collins is able to pull off this trick courtesy of his big time sponsorships with the USFSA and Skate Canada.

Collins winds up with an endless supply of talent, and *Stars on Ice*, as a rule, has to wait for North American skaters to turn professional.

The two tours are competitive on other fronts, too.

Seeing how the *Stars on Ice* show was booming in the 1990s with its popular ensemble numbers, Tom Collins called on 1979 World Pair Champion-turned-choreographer Randy Gardner. First, to spruce up his opening and closing numbers where each skater has a brief highlight, and then eventually to create an ensemble number to close Act One.

Despite their warm history—Randy and partner Tai Babilonia had toured with Tom Collins on several occasions, and their agent was his good friend Rosenberg—it was not all smiles. Actually, it was downright exasperating for Randy.

"The thing is, Tommy had no management of the skaters. He still doesn't. And I was used to, and still am used to, a schedule, a running order before we go in, a concept, plus everybody's required to do rehearsal situation," explains Randy.

"So I got there and had none of that. Other than, I knew what the opening thing was, I knew what the closing thing was. You get there, half the cast is there, it's very disorganized."

According to Randy, Collins doesn't tell the skaters what to expect or impress upon them the importance of taking the rehearsals seriously.

"The skaters all come in with their own preconceived notion of what they're going to do. And they don't want to do that much. So they come in, you're all there, and they're talking, they're eating lunch, they're running around, they're screaming. There was no rehearsal responsibility with that cast at all," declares Randy.

"You're confronted with a group of skaters that are very talented, but not wanting to do much and not wanting to be told what to do. So it's a challenge. You're running after them, trying to find them, because they're not there, instead they're back at the hotel. It's very tough. We wasted a lot of time. There was no feedback at all from Tommy. The entire situation was very frustrating."

Randy worked as the choreographer on the Collins tours for two years. Starting with the 1999 summer tour, he was replaced by Sarah Kawahara, Michelle Kwan's current choreographer.

What was so upsetting for Randy was that Collins never mentioned a word to him personally about the decision. Instead, the news came from Rosenberg, who merely listed it as one of the things he wanted to talk about with Randy over dinner one night. Seemingly, everyone was in the loop but Randy.

"It got me in my stomach. This was in July, and that tour had started the beginning of April. And I had been out with my maintenance stops all throughout every month and didn't hear anything," muses Randy. So he confronted Collins.

"I said, 'Tommy, I hear you're looking for someone else to do my job.' And he said yes. He was very cavalier. He didn't say why. He said, 'I'm going for a new approach, not that I'm not going to use you, I'm just going for a new approach.' I asked if there was anything wrong with my work. He said no, everything I did was fine," offers Randy.

Oddly enough, Collins wanted Randy to remain on for the 1999 winter tour. "I almost said no. But I went and did it that following January just out of professional reasons and to make him look more silly," contends Randy.

"He wanted to do something different. That's fine. However, I've known Tommy for 20-something years. The biggest part of it is that I would have liked to have been told directly by him when he made the decision.

"I didn't care about the job. I liked it and would like to have still done the job. But I went on to do other things anyway. It was all personal to me. It wasn't professional at all. We haven't spoken since," Randy says.

As for the backstage atmosphere, Randy reports a lot of small separate cliques exist and that the touring life doesn't always bring out the best in people.

"The true personalities come out, because they're traveling and they're tired. I never understood the grumpy ones, because they were being paid so well. I still don't get that. But when it's over for them, they'll think back and go, 'Oh,'" quips Randy.

"It's really difficult, because you do spend four months out of your life with these same people. You have to find a level of understanding with everyone, and everyone is different," admits 1995 U.S. Women's Champion Nicole Bobek, a long-time *Champions on Ice* cast member.

"The thing I've learned over the years is that you have to have respect for everyone, because we all do the same kind of work out there," she adds. "We just handle things differently. There's no escaping it, you have to see these people every single day. Emotionally, we all get tired, and women have their periods and other things like that. You just have to deal with it."

The 2002 post-Olympic tour, which ran from April until August, was particularly grueling, admits veteran Rudy Galindo.

"Sure, it does get hard, because you hit walls. It's just like everyday life or everyday work. You get up in the morning and say, 'Oh my God, how do I do this?' But then you have to tell yourself that this is a job that you enjoy very much and are privileged to do," he says.

Joining Rudy and the others on the trek across America were Sarah Hughes and her Salt Lake City teammate, Sasha Cohen. Both have discovered that life on the road isn't easy when you're so young.

"I think it is a little difficult for Sarah and Sasha, because they do try to fit in and have conversations with the 30-year-olds on the tour," assesses Rudy. "They try to learn where they can fit in and what kind of adult conversations they can join. You can tell, though, that it's a little hard on them."

Nicole agrees, but believes the balance of new and seasoned tour members is a plus. "Sure, it's difficult for them," she says. "Yet they're so young, so free. They really look up to us and respect the older skaters, especially the professionals. We look up to them, too, because they are inspiring—so driven, so into what they do—and are so competitive that it pushes us."

Collins declined numerous requests to be interviewed for *Frozen Assets* to discuss the skaters, his background, the current state of his tour, his future plans for it and his enterprise at large. In fact, he stormed out of a scheduled interview insisting he was telling his story in his own book commemorating 25 years of *Champions on Ice*.

Nevertheless, with the formation of Collins Marshall Management, for which Tom Collins is the CEO, the battle between titans Tom Collins Enterprises and IMG is obviously escalating beyond the tours.

Eventually, Collins wants to give IMG a run for its money in not only skater representation, but also event producing.

He will have a long way to go to catch IMG, which has been involved in these aspects of figure skating for more than two decades.

IMG's interest in skating started rather modestly in the late 1970s and early 1980s with the representation of two Olympic bronze medalists: American Janet Lynn, considered one of the sport's best-ever free skaters, and Toller Cranston, the flamboyant and creative Canadian.

Then in 1983, IMG realized skating was on its way to becoming a big-time Olympic sport and wanted to get in on the ground level.

Bob Kain, who had been running the company's booming tennis business, along with senior vice president Jay Ogden, who had been managing Toller, took on the task of building a figure skating platform. Remarkably, they had no real strategy in place, says Kain.

"We thought it was a good television sport and the Olympics

were going to keep making it a more important sport, because it was the thing America was reasonably good at, and they had to keep pumping it. So we thought American television would drive it, and the Olympics would drive it," explains Kain. "We thought it was going to be international, and that would measure up with what we were doing in tennis and golf."

Kain's first introduction to skating—even before going to an event—came in the living room of Rosalynn Sumners, who was the 1983 World Women's Champion and, ironically, today is his fiancée.

"I went in there with Jay, and we tried to sign her, and her parents said we were great. Then three months later, we got a call saying they were going with Lee Mimms, who represented Peggy Fleming," recalls Kain.

"So seven or eight years later, when Roz is skating on *Stars on Ice*, I said, 'When you were recruited by IMG, why didn't you sign with them?' And she said, 'I wasn't comfortable with the guy who did all the talking.' She thought it was Jay, but it was me. When I told her that, she couldn't believe it."

A little later on, Kain had better luck with Scott Hamilton, who had just won the 1984 Olympics and World Championships.

"Scott went with me because one of his sports heroes was Bjorn Borg, and I managed Bjorn Borg. So Scott said, 'Come with me, we're going to Atlantic City, we're going to announce that I'm turning professional and you're going to be my guy,'" shares Kain.

Little did Kain know at the time, but from this relationship would rise the IMG figure skating dynasty.

"IMG looked at skating as a professional sport that was really nowhere. My goal was to try and see if we could build this sport pretty much like we had done in tennis and golf, which was to manage the superstars and promote events if the opportunities arose. Certainly the television events, and maybe some exhibitions, and do the television production," states Kain.

It fascinated Kain that the U.S. skating superstars of the 1984 Olympics were on the cover of *Sports Illustrated* one minute, then instantly forgotten when they turned professional.

Yet that was the way the figure skating structure was at the time. In fact, then-professionals like Scott Hamilton were not allowed to be on the same ice as Olympic-eligible skaters, even in an exhibition show like the Tom Collins tour. So Scott joined *Ice Capades*, only to be dismissed two years later when *Ice Capades* changed hands. The new owner said they couldn't justify Hamilton's salary, because male skaters don't sell tickets.

Kain saw a clear opportunity for a niche that could be filled.

"Skaters like Scott couldn't do any competitions, couldn't be on exhibition tours. And these were the biggest stars in the sport, and they're treated like outcasts. So we decided to build a professional sport around them and generate our own work," recalls Kain.

That quickly became a reality.

Starting in 1980, IMG partnered with Dick Button in the World Professional Figure Skating Championships, a competition aired on NBC. In 1984, they began to launch other competitions and shows.

What would be IMG's ultimate claim to fame in the sport came in 1986.

The jumpstart, ironically, for *Stars on Ice* was a low point for Scott—his termination from *Ice Capades*.

"They said, 'Goodbye, thank you very much,' and 'You can come back at a fraction of your salary, and we have one week for you next year.' I thought, *That's not where I want to be next year.* And I was panicked, because it was only two years into my career and I felt like I was being fired," recalls Hamilton, who had never missed an *Ice Capades* performance or press call.

The notion of creating a tour fit the need at the time, says

Scott. "I looked at the number of marquee skaters that were out there and saw stars that were either underappreciated or not given the opportunities that I felt they really deserved to develop careers of their own. They really needed an opportunity to be stars in their own right. And I just felt like the audience was sophisticated in the skating more than ever before, because ratings were better for television," he reasons.

"The 1984 Olympics produced huge TV numbers, and a lot of big stories came out of it: Jayne Torvill & Christopher Dean, Katarina Witt, Roz, myself and Brian Orser. Plus Kitty & Peter Carruthers did extremely well and almost won the pair event, and ice dancers Judy Blumberg & Michael Seibert were phenomenal. I thought, we have a really solid depth, so we should be able to present that on a professional level."

Kain, who co-founded the tour with Scott, says, at the time, the show was quite a risk. "We started out in these little dinky towns in New England. Scott had wanted to start out like the Tom Collins tour and play in front of 15,000 people at Madison Square Garden, but we had to build up to that," he explains.

Kain had envisioned the tour to be like a winter version of the Collins tour, a place for pro skaters such as Brian Boitano and Katarina Witt to turn to in 1988 after they concluded their amateur careers.

That didn't happen for several reasons.

"It quickly became evident that our plan was right on target, because by 1988, all of the rules changed, and professionals could skate on the Tom Collins tour. Tom certainly understood if the pros can't skate on his tour, they were all going to end up on *Stars on Ice*," states Kain.

"We wished people hadn't caught on quite so fast. But in that four year period, as I've often said to Scott, we changed the whole landscape of skating. We changed all the rules, and we changed all of the post-Olympic career opportunities, which was pretty cool. And Scott was the driving force behind that."

After the initial few years it took to establish *Stars on Ice*, the tour enjoyed a solid level of success.

Scott had imparted to the tour's cast a key philosophy he had learned from former *Ice Capades* president Dick Palmer. "Ice skating is glamorous. If you're having a bad day or horrible travel or you're stuck in a bad hotel, nobody in the world wants to hear that," he advises. "They're coming to you to take a couple hours off from their problems. So respect your audience."

Then things got even better in the 1992–93 season, when a new creative team and production staff came on board. How that new staff landed at IMG is an interesting little tale.

The *Stars on Ice* that people know today—the one of state-of-the-art lighting and sound, exquisite costumes and a top notch creative team—came courtesy of the *Skating* tours, starring Brian Boitano and Katarina Witt, that ran from 1990–92.

Skating, presented by Bill Graham Productions, was the forerunner of the Broadway-type ice show with theatrical lighting and entertaining ensembles, but it had trouble turning a profit.

"We were never able to get to where we made money. I think in the last tour we started to break even, but, unfortunately, there was this horrible accident with Bill Graham (he died in a helicopter crash)," explains Katarina. "Basically, he did the tour for the love of the sport, or he just wanted to do something outside of the rock 'n' roll shows he produced. He loved the idea. Maybe if the accident hadn't happened, our tour would have taken a different path."

Instead, the *Skating* production was put on the block, and IMG bought it.

"The truth is, *Stars on Ice* had the chance at it and grabbed it.

A lot of people who started something special with us then went to IMG. But that's business, which is hard to take, but that's just part of it," reasons Katarina.

Creative director Sandra Bezic, choreographer Michael Seibert, lighting director Ken Billington and various other technical and creative staff were instantly with *Stars on Ice*.

"For me, it was the first time I understood how capitalism works. There were financial and marketing decisions made which broke my heart as performer," offers Katarina. "Ultimately, I think if Brian and I had a better business idea, the tour may not have gotten sold."

Regardless, Katarina completely understood Bezic's decision. "She's an artist, she's a choreographer and a director and she wanted to work. For me, it's totally understandable that she didn't want to sit there and twiddle her thumbs and, instead, would go with *Stars on Ice*."

It was harder for Brian Boitano to take. "It's definitely something that broke Brian's heart more than mine, because I then joined *Stars* and he never did," notes Katarina.

While the production values of *Stars on Ice* increased with the addition of the *Skating* brain trust, it proved an adjustment for the skaters and existing staff.

"In the early years, along with Karen Kresge, who was the director and choreographer, we, the skaters, all really pitched in. It's where I got a lot of my experience doing choreography," says Lea Ann Miller, who was with *Stars* from its inception—first as a skater and then as a choreographer—until the conclusion of the 2000–01 season.

"I sort of came from the old school, and it was an adapting process to Sandra's ways. It still was a team effort. We met in Toronto, where Sandra lives, and brainstormed ideas. It was always a collaboration and a delegation of which choreographer was doing what number. At this point, the skaters probably had less input into the show than they did in the earlier years."

"*Stars on Ice* started out as the skaters' tour. It was our ideas; we would collaborate, and together, we would make it a great show. It was exciting to see it come together on opening night. It was our baby," says Brian Orser, who performed with *Stars on Ice* for seven years (1988–94 and 1998–99), and continued to perform with *Stars on Ice Canada* through 2002.

"Now, it's a little bit different, for various reasons, and skaters are not involved as much anymore. They're just kind of told what the show is and where they're skating, where they're standing and what they're wearing. There are some skaters who prefer it that way, but there are some skaters who want to be more involved, and would like to be part of the creative development. That's the way *Stars* used to be, and it was a lot of fun."

Overall though, he has been thrilled with the show's development over the years. "It's really cool to see where the show has gone. From a U-Haul truck to three major trucks on the U.S. tour for equipment and props. And from a bus for the skaters to a private jet."

The process of putting a show like *Stars on Ice* together is a long one for Sandra Bezic and her team. They start working on the next year's tour before the current one is even finished.

"Every year, Michael Seibert, Christopher Dean and I sit down with (costume designer) Jef Billings to discuss what we've done, where we've been and where the skaters should be going or could be going," shares Bezic. "We also talk about what's going on in the world and what kind of musical sounds are currently out there. Michael, Chris and I listen to music endlessly, and that process triggers ideas. It's a giant jigsaw puzzle that slowly begins to form.

"Our intention is always to produce each skater as individual stars, but also use the power of the group. And probably the most challenging thing is to come up with something fresh each year and have a fresh way of looking at things. What we do try to do is break our formula each year and do something different," says Bezic.

When it comes to the skaters' solo numbers, the creative team stays right on top of that, too. "Over the summer, we are in touch with the skaters to see what their ideas are. They, in turn, listen to us and see what our ideas are for them. Then they take that away, whether we choreograph it for them, someone else does or they do it themselves," offers Dean.

While Bezic has done wonderful work in her decade with the show, last season's creative effort—*Moulin Rouge* meets The Carpenters' music—went over like a lead balloon.

"It was too sophisticated. Once in a while everyone makes mistakes," says Orser. "There was definitely a blip in the growth and development of the show last year.

"Sandra had to incorporate ways of giving the three Olympic ladies' champions (Tara Lipinski, Kristi Yamaguchi and Katarina Witt) equal time on the ice. It was a real challenge, and it didn't work out. With some of the ensemble numbers, she got carried away."

The creative aspect being off the mark wasn't the only thing people noticed. It was the first tour without Scott Hamilton. And the show felt the loss.

While *Champions on Ice* was buoyed by its post-Olympic tour of new medalists, *Stars on Ice* was hit hard in early 2002, as attendance fell by a staggering 40 to 50 percent.

"When Scott was in the show, he was in charge, and he was going between the cast and IMG and telling the people what he needed for the show and for the people. He was the crazy glue between all those people, and right now, it is like he was never there," assesses Oksana Baiul. "I felt like all the skaters were skating so much better than they had been, but the show was not really good."

Tour producer Byron Allen agrees in part—Scott's absence was palpable. "Certainly all of the Q-ratings and those type of things list him at the top of popular figure skaters, probably of all time. You couldn't help but miss him," Allen acknowledges. He also believes the poor economy was a big factor in declining ticket sales.

"This past year, with the next generation of *Stars* taking over the tour, it was inevitable that it was going to be an adjustment period. Not only for the audience, but for the skaters as well," offers Scott. "I think this year will be phenomenal year. We're going to have some of the new Olympians coming in, which will add a new look and feel to the tour, as the last one with Tara [Lipinski] and Ilia [Kulik]."

Scott says that when you look at the most successful seasons for *Stars on Ice*, the show was driven by factors beyond skating. "A lot of the peak years for *Stars on Ice* have been when people had more than just a skating interest in the show. They had kind of an emotional investment in seeing the show: the year that Katia [Gordeeva] came back, the year I came back from cancer," he explains.

"All those years gave people more of a reason to go out and see something beyond just seeing a skating show. Those were the years where you're bringing in more than the skating fans."

Despite the downward slide last year, Kain takes great pride in how far the tour has come. "The first year we did this, the precursor of what *Stars on Ice* is today, we went to Philadelphia and took in $17,000. After we played Philadelphia in Scott's final year, we had ticket sales of $680,000. It was a pretty good improvement!"

When asked how best to distinguish between *Stars* and *Champions on Ice*, Kain recalls a conversation he once shared with Christopher Dean on the very subject.

"Christopher said, '*Stars* is our work and our livelihood, and *Champions* is a vacation after our work.' And there's nothing wrong with that. If you work hard at the U.S. Championships and the World Championships, you're ready for a vacation," offers Kain. "Christopher said, 'I don't want to skate one number, I want to come out and work, and this is the way I'm going to keep improving my craft.' That's what *Stars on Ice* is all about."

In fact, that description would apply to the personalities of many people at IMG. Instead of Tom Collins' style of jeans and cowboy boots, they wear suits and ties. All are college graduates, and most have advanced degrees in either law or business. They view skating as a business, as opposed to a big family—a style that is abundantly satisfactory for some and not desirable for others.

Though it is the most sought after gig, *Stars on Ice* is by no means the only work opportunity IMG generates for its clients today.

IMG is behind the only head-to-head pro competition, the Hallmark Skaters' Championship, and, through its partnership with Steve Disson's company, has seven made-for-television exhibitions.

There's no way to overstate it. IMG is the consistent thread that runs throughout professional skating, so work comes oh-so-much easier if you're in its fold.

"IMG (with Disson Skating) owns and operates all of the professional exhibitions and events. I would tend to think that the skaters realize that we're their source of income, so they do it for the money that is available. What's the alternative? They could coach or pick up some one-off club shows. If they want to continue to skate, they take what they are offered," says one insider involved with the productions.

The IMG clients are primarily the thoroughbreds of figure skating. Besides Scott Hamilton, IMG represents Kristi Yamaguchi, Ekaterina Gordeeva, Kurt Browning, Todd Eldredge and Alexei Yagudin.

The IMG ride, however, isn't always a smooth one, cautions Toller Cranston. "IMG is only after the top, so what happens is the IMG clients make the mistake of thinking the IMG employees are their friends," he proclaims.

"But there is a stable there, and they will change your stall if a new winner comes in. Then all of a sudden you can't say, 'But, but, I'm so-and-so.' It is like, 'Get out of here.' You are not in *Stars on Ice* anymore, or you're not invited to such and such event."

IMG would argue: that's just business.

As figure skating has increasingly come back to earth the last few years, and the inflated expectations have lifted, everyone still standing in skating is laying claim to what's theirs.

For IMG, that's the professional arena.

"We're definitely going to be the protector of professional skating. We will fight very hard anyone and everyone who tries to stop that," declares Kain.

"Our business has been driven by listening to our athletes, and I think that's still going to be the case. The new group, if you will, the Todd Eldredges and Alexei Yagudins, these guys are going to want to have careers, and we're going to make sure that they do."

If the new crop of skating talent is going to enjoy success anywhere near that of the sport's heyday, the two studios are going to have to get with the times, says Brian Boitano.

"They need to be visionaries instead of reactionary. The world is constantly evolving, and our sport stays the same. It needs to roll with what happens in the world," he argues.

Rosenberg is more precise. "In today's economy, ticket prices for ice skating shows are extremely expensive—comparable to off-Broadway and Broadway shows. They are not family-friendly priced," he assesses. "The tours have to find ways to remedy this and to cut their costs. They will have to, in order to survive."

Takeover

5

"Companies were bought coming off of very good years when earnings were high. Skating had experienced a great period where business was good, television numbers were real, tour dates sold a lot of tickets and skaters earned a lot of money."

– Lee Marshall,
President of Collins Marshall Management
(formerly of Magicworks
and SFX Family Entertainment)

Takeover

Professional figure skating was once a hot commodity, indeed.

Entrepreneurs, eager to jump on the bandwagon and pay top dollar for the ride, led a flurry of consolidations—all with the vision of rivaling the skating monopoly called IMG.

But when the dust finally settled on these takeovers, instead of creating a market foe for IMG, they had eliminated all the competition and laid it at IMG's feet.

Along the way, it was curtains for several fixtures of the skating world.

Gone was the venerable World Professional Figure Skating Championships. Gone was one of the leading talent agencies for figure skaters. And when these deals went through, out went the creative and driving force of their founders, Dick Button and Michael Rosenberg.

How did it all go so horribly wrong?

By its nature, a takeover is unpredictable. What the buyer says will be done with the company and what actually happens are often two different things. Good intentions fall by the wayside as business needs and the economy change.

Simply put, when public demand for the sport dropped sharply, all bets were off.

Not to be overlooked is the role that the ISU and USFSA played. The two most powerful organizations in eligible skating were always concerned that the independent promoters of professional events were going to take skaters out of the Olympic system and sign them to lucrative pro contracts. When skating boomed in the mid-1990s, this fear escalated to near panic proportions. The ISU and USFSA dug in their heels and made promoters pay exorbitant fees to get events sanctioned—which would allow eligible skaters to participate—if they sanctioned them at all.

Seeing the handwriting on the wall, Button, Rosenberg and others got out while the getting was good—very good.

Sold for $7 million: Michael Rosenberg's Marco Entertainment, Inc.

Sold for $8 million: Dick Button's Candid Productions.

Sold for undisclosed millions: Jefferson Pilot Sports Figure Skating.

Sold for $100 million: Magicworks Entertainment.

The sale that got the ball rolling was Marco Entertainment to Magicworks Entertainment in August 1998.

Magicworks, headed by Lee Marshall, was a big-time player in the production and promotion of live entertainment events, including theatrical shows, music concerts and skating events. It also provided representation and sports marketing services to professional athletes. Marco did primarily the same thing, only exclusively in figure skating.

"It seemed great. The people at Magicworks were very enthusiastic and real skating fans. Together, we had many, many plans," says Michael Rosenberg, founder of Marco. "Then, within 30 days of that purchase being finalized, SFX bought Magicworks."

SFX, a leading promoter, producer and marketer of live entertainment events, wanted to expand the interests and reach of its sports marketing group. The goal was to create a winter sports division similar to that of powerhouse IMG.

Marshall moved with Magicworks and became the president and chief operating officer of the SFX Family Entertainment division, which housed figure skating.

"SFX had great enthusiasm for skating, and they were very promotionally minded and gambling oriented. They were promoter type personalities. We were all ultra excited," recalls Rosenberg, who also remained on board as part of his original deal with Magicworks.

The SFX buying spree was only beginning.

It acquired Jefferson Pilot Sports Figure Skating, whose biggest claim to fame was the pro team competition called Ice Wars.

The man behind the figure skating push at Jefferson Pilot was Mike Burg. He had a simple, yet winning, notion in the early 1990s. "Hey, there is not a lot of skating on television right now. If we can get the big personalities, we probably can create some television around them."

So Jefferson Pilot selectively entered into alliances with certain skaters. Tara Lipinski was handled for athlete representation. Both Katarina Witt and Oksana Baiul had contracts for appearances. All of them are Olympic Champions tailor-made for easy sells to the networks.

Jefferson Pilot's emergence was a thorn in IMG's side. Burg recalls an intense meeting with CBS that also included IMG.

"CBS said they were going to split their inventory between us and IMG because they didn't want to piss off anybody," Burg says. "They didn't want to annoy Jefferson Pilot, because they owned some big stations, and they certainly didn't want to annoy IMG, because they had so many other desirable sports products for the network. Obviously, each of us had wanted it all."

Jefferson Pilot, however, didn't put all of its eggs in the CBS basket. Beginning in 1994, and running for three years on FOX, was the Rock and Roll Figure Skating Championships. The first installment, starring Oksana Baiul and Nancy Kerrigan, is still the highest rated non-Olympic skating show in prime-time television.

Also under the Jefferson Pilot umbrella was the Legends competition from 1995–98, the *Too Hot to Skate* outdoor shows and a few other one-time efforts—including the 1999 ESPN Pro Championships that marked Tonya Harding's first and only entrée into pro skating.

SFX put the final feather in its skating cap in July 1999 with the purchase of Dick Button's Candid Productions, which was responsible for the most prestigious pro competition: the World Professional Figure Skating Championships.

Also commonly called "Landover," for the city in Maryland in which it was held for many years, this event started out in a team format, but in 1983 introduced the individual disciplines. Invitations were coveted to the competition, and it became a vehicle for accelerating careers and creating rivalries, such as Brian Boitano versus Kurt Browning.

Candid Productions also produced the U.S. Professional Championships, the Challenge of Champions and the World Team Championships.

"I felt the timing was right. I sold it for no other reason than that I've been doing skating events for 40 years. We did the first ones that were on television. I quite think that span was enough," insists Button.

A huge company like SFX coming in gave high hopes to the Candid Productions' staff—which was retained in the merger—that the grass would only get greener.

"We thought SFX could do the time-buys with the television networks, and the events would continue," recalls Craig Cichy, associate producer at Candid Productions. "We gave them all of this information to help secure sponsors, plus other historical information on the events themselves, so they could have their people go out and secure sponsors so the events would get produced and on the air."

But SFX failed to follow through.

This inaction wasn't all that unpredictable, attests Rosenberg. "With all the corporate red tape, it took five sign-offs on anything to get it done."

This culture was a big change for him and the others who used to call the shots and make things happen.

Declares Cichy, "After that first year that SFX was our boss, we could clearly tell that the support just wasn't there for skating and [that] they weren't going to bend over backward to help get us sponsors. It seemed like their interest in skating went completely out the window."

Of the four events Candid Productions had established, only the World Professional Championships took place after the SFX deal.

"I don't know why SFX didn't get behind skating and these events. I just never understood why on earth they bought all these entities if they were just going to let everything fizzle," remarks Cichy.

"Once SFX accumulated a lot of pieces and parts in the figure skating business, I don't really feel like they produced to the level that they had been producing traditionally over the last five years," assesses Marshall. "When you analyze that against all the money they spent accumulating it, it paled in comparison.

"When the numbers didn't pan out, I think that they re-evaluated and made a decision that they were going to scale back their figure skating division."

The disintegration of the Candid events and the blood, sweat and tears that went into them was a bitter pill to swallow for Button and his staff.

"Dick was so sad that SFX let it all go. It was really frustrating for him, because he was hoping, too, that they would take the ball and run with it and make World Pro, in particular, really super and keep the event going and going," offers Cichy.

The bloom came completely off the rose in June 2000 when SFX was purchased by Clear Channel Communications, the biggest radio station operator in the world, which did not have figure skating on its to-do list.

"When Clear Channel bought SFX, the folks who had bought my company had left," explains Marshall. "So the people who had the vision I got excited about were no longer at the company."

Instead, Clear Channel had their eyes trained on SFX's other entities—most notably, the gold mine tie-in of their radio stations with the promotions of SFX live music events, as well as the immediately more profitable areas of auto racing and team sports.

In the final analysis, it simply proved very poor timing to turn over the livelihood of these annual skating events to outsiders to the sport. Simultaneously, with skating's popularity starting on a major decline, there was no one left in charge with a passion for skating to fight for it.

When the television networks declined to automatically renew the competitions, the ball was in Clear Channel's court. The networks offered Clear Channel the rights to buy the time and sell it to advertisers on its own. Clear Channel passed.

"Clear Channel simply declined to gamble," declares Rosenberg. "They kept saying to Dick and myself that now is not the time. We were horribly frustrated. This meant Dick was left with no competitions, and my aspirations of regular tours and theatrical shows were gone.

"It's a case of different priorities. Figure skating was just a little blip on the radar screen, barely on the radar screen. So Clear Channel was unable to give us the green light on all our plans, hopes and dreams," he adds.

Of all the events SFX/Clear Channel acquired in their purchases, only Jefferson Pilot's Ice Wars is still in existence and televised.

Dick Button's management contract with SFX/Clear Channel for the operation of Candid Productions came to an end in 2001, when the company bought out the remaining eight months.

"The deal was for three years, and I didn't want to continue. When I fell and fractured my skull (December 31, 2000), I had a chance to do a lot of thinking. I was not interested in continuing on with it. I had been there, done that. I want to continue to develop and move into new, intriguing areas," explains Button.

Interestingly, Button's parting deal with Clear Channel included the return of ownership rights to the World Professional Figure Skating Championships, which was last held in December 2000. Basically, Button has the competition name back, which he can sell to a promoter.

As the professional events quickly dwindled, one person jumped at the chance to fill the vacuum.

It was Steve Disson, a sports-marketing executive and event producer whose ties with figure skating began with the *Sudafed*

Skating and Gymnastics Spectacular in 1989. Three years later he took on various deal-making responsibilities with the USFSA.

Disson helped the USFSA introduce their fall and spring open events (where both professional and eligible skaters compete) by bringing on board sponsors, such as Hershey's, Chrysler, AT&T and the U.S. Postal Service, and securing television time.

"The USFSA management asked us, 'What would it take to get your clients involved in these events?' They listened, and then we got it done," relates Disson. "It was the idea of one-stop shopping, in which corporations could come in and title sponsor one USFSA event and then be a support sponsor of the other events."

Fast forward to 1999. Seeing an opportunity with pro skating fading fast from the air, he and then–business partner Allen Furst expanded and created Disson Furst and Partners. The goal was for the company to be extensively involved in figure skating and also have projects going in other areas, such as cycling and motor sports.

Disson's forte of buying airtime from networks and selling sponsorships made him the right man for the job—the job that no one else was willing to do.

In 1999, after promising prior collaborations, Disson and England-based Adventure! on Ice, the company owned by 1980 Olympic Men's Champion Robin Cousins and former British Ice Dance Champion Nicky Slater, partnered on a new skating series for NBC called *StarSkates*.

The four shows were theme-based on a particular type of music, such as Latin or country.

"They were great in the sense that we had some wonderful talent and some creative shows, but we found that the name *StarSkates* didn't mean anything to the general public. What means something to them is Brian Boitano's name or Scott

Hamilton's or Kristi Yamaguchi's. Skating shows are name driven. It was really tough to brand *StarSkates*," admits Disson.

Slater, who was front and center in the shows' creation, had failed to understand the U.S. market. Worse yet, under his direction, the events were poorly executed—and some were an all-out disaster.

Without a doubt, the best example of the blundering was the 2000 *StarSkates Latin* event. Slater had inexplicably gotten the run time wrong. The show came up a whopping 20 minutes short upon arrival at the production office for editing and packaging.

"It was just criminally short, so much so that we basically put in every interview, and there was a look back at previous *StarSkates*, and there was a look forward at every single *StarSkates*, simply to fill time," quips a production person from the show.

From choreography to scheduling, these events were low in quality and control across the board, insists the insider.

"Choreographer Lea Ann Miller (hired to assist with choreography, as Cousins had his leg in a cast in the autumn of 2000) tried her best," notes the insider. "She came prepared, and everybody was fighting her. It was like hitting your head against a wall. People wouldn't show up for rehearsal, people would fly in at the last minute. Skaters need a firm hand even if they are professionals, and nobody was giving it to them. Skaters were wandering around. It was just sloppy.

"Nicky kept putting out new schedules, but apparently they were only for him. He would hang it on the door of his office, but not make sure the skaters and everybody else saw it. Scheduling was a big part of what he was supposed to do, and that was just a perpetual mess."

It seems nobody was keeping an eye on the ball as far as production, and nobody was making anybody do anything.

"Nicky should have been the hands-on official. Robin was the creative guy, and Steve took care of the TV buys," assesses the insider.

Disson wised up and parted ways with Adventure! on Ice.

In 2001, largely due to the lack of prosperity with the figure skating ventures, Disson Furst and Partners also disbanded. Disson took the event sponsorship and skating entities with him and formed two new companies: Disson and Associates, a corporate sponsorship match-up service, and Disson Skating. Furst retained the interests in the other sports.

In need of financial muscle for his skating expansion to fully pan out, Disson joined forces with IMG. In turn, IMG gained more employment opportunities for its skaters, who now dominate the lineup at all Disson-produced events.

Confident that a successful skating series was quite viable, Disson went back to the concept that made the most sense: building a show around one major star.

He had done this for a few years already with Brian Boitano's annual event, so he knew it would work.

That season, Disson/IMG produced six such shows that aired on NBC, each at cost of roughly a million dollars. In 2002, they expanded to seven shows for the network.

"We pay for the TV production, all the skaters, the set, the lighting—for everything. Where the money is made back is through the sale of sponsorships and commercial spots," Disson explains. "With the economy the way it's been the last couple of years, we're probably the only ones gutsy enough to do the time buys, because there's a lot of risk involved. They are totally dependent upon sponsorships."

"Working with creative skating partners and bringing in musical artists for a tribute show has made for a great formula. Skaters like to skate for Kurt Browning in his show and Kristi in her show. And the public likes these stars. We've found our own little niche," says Disson.

The USFSA, however, has not made it easy, even for Disson, who was integral in bringing major sponsors to the organization. At the root of the issue is the USFSA's multi-million dollar contract with ABC for the broadcast of eligible events. Within this deal is a "slush fund" for appearance fees for the skaters.

According to Burg, who was Tara Lipinski's agent during her eligible days, top U.S. skaters can get $150,000 each to do an event like Skate America, regardless of their final placement.

The objective is to provide the top U.S. skaters with enough money that they will do USFSA events exclusively on ABC and not turn pro. Therefore, any event on a major network like NBC or CBS is seen as a direct conflict by the USFSA, so they hesitate to sanction it for their skaters.

"ABC has paid a lot of money for a package of skating, programs, and the USFSA wants to keep that deal healthy. As a result, the USFSA doesn't even want their skaters appearing in non-competitions [on other networks]. The governing body is trying to become a monopoly," states Bob Kain, President and COO, Americas, IMG.

"We're a private company, we can squeeze out the competition. But the USFSA should not."

According to unnamed sources, IMG did win one round against the USFSA during the past Olympic season when Todd Eldredge was allowed to participate in one of the Disson/IMG shows. Kristi Yamaguchi, who is good friends with Todd (having been on the 1992 U.S. Olympic team together), threatened to not do one of the USFSA events unless Todd was allowed to do the show she was headlining for Disson/IMG. Left with no choice, the USFSA caved.

The Disson/IMG shows are not even competitions, and their live dates and telecast dates don't conflict with USFSA events. "We were sanctioned in the past when we only had one or two events, but as we've gotten bigger in numbers, the USFSA began to look at us as its competition. The skaters want to do our events instead, even for less money, because they are not competitions and they like our creative partner who we have with us. They are fun shows to do," states Disson.

"We constantly talk to the USFSA about getting a sanction or exemption. Sometimes they cooperate, and sometimes they don't."

Stepping into the skating fray in early 2002 was Collins Marshall Management (CMM), the brainchild of Lee Marshall and *Champions on Ice* tour manager Michael Collins. CMM provides management and marketing services to figure skaters and also has its sights set on producing events.

"The level of interest in skating will fluctuate from year to year, but there are always skaters who need to be represented in a personal, one-on-one way. That's how Lee and I handle things," says Michael Collins.

"There are too many skaters and not enough options for them as to where to go for representation. Figure skating is going to be around forever. Somebody else needs to be in the marketplace."

Sound familiar?

Skates For Hire

"In 1994, we all knew that it was a huge buzz of craziness. We thought it was great, because it was stirring up new interest. We thought the good events and competitions would survive, the bad ones would go away, but the popularity of skating would still increase. We knew it was a wave to ride. We were hoping to keep it going as much and as long as possible."

– Kristi Yamaguchi,
1992 Olympic and World Women's Champion

Skates for Hire

During the glory days of pro skating, money and opportunities in the limelight abounded for all—be they Olympic or World Champions, national medalists or relative unknowns.

That's a far cry from the scene today.

The parade of annual, televised pro competitions is no more. And if you're not a skating superstar or don't have the right connections, you might find yourself scrambling for work or doing things you thought were beneath you.

For the skating elite—the ones on either of the premier tours, *Champions on Ice* or *Stars on Ice*—times are still good. Only not as insanely good as during the mid- to late-1990s, when money flowed freely and top stars commanded six figure paydays as a guarantee for a single night's work.

In contrast, for each of the seven Steve Disson/IMG exhibition specials on NBC, the total payout for the cast of eight to 12 skaters is between $120,000 and $160,000. In the sport's heyday, a top skater could get that, or more, for a single event.

The superstars have no room to complain, however, because for everyone else, the current picture isn't nearly as pretty.

At skating's peak, skaters like former U.S. Women's silver medalist Tonia Kwiatkowski and former French Champion and two-time Olympian Eric Millot competed in various events and made many appearances. Now they find themselves doing more coaching than performing, because the pay is better—and they're more in demand for it. Plus, as a coach, you don't have to live a taxing, nomadic existence venturing to all parts of the globe for work.

As the opportunities have dwindled across the board, skaters in the second and third tiers of success must decide how badly they want to skate, because it won't be easy, and it won't be comfortable. Try performing in front of small crowds at theme parks—where the story is the star, not you—at tank shows or on plastic ice that seems the size of a postage stamp, be it on a cruise ship or elsewhere out of the norm. Or try barely seeing your home as you endure nonstop, far-flung travel.

There is one exception to this gloom and doom: get a gimmick! Have acrobatic skills or a hula-hoop, and the work will come. Skaters with a gimmick, with no credentials from Olympic-style competition and with limited skating experience in general, will get work over the likes of Kwiatkowski and Millot, because they're a novelty. Never mind the fact that they won't be doing any jumps or some of the other moves one expects to see from skaters.

Vladimir Besedin and Alexei Polishuk, aptly nicknamed The Acrobats, have been performing their strongman duet in *Champions on Ice* for several years now. Irina Gregorian, The Hula-Hoop Girl, who previously plied her trade in a Las Vegas stage show, was added to the tour this past season.

Stars on Ice, which had been known for having only the best skaters in the world, also got into this trend last year when they added Lucinda Ruh, the Swiss Women's Champion who can spin far better than she can do anything else. In her solo program for *Stars on Ice*, Ruh never jumped a single time. She has also been invited to the skating season's only head-to-head competition.

So Ruh, who never placed in the medals at any major eligible competition, was on skating's most exclusive tour. And whose place did she take? That of 1994 World Women's Champion and multiple pro competition winner Yuka Sato, who is known for her superior quality and who is often called a skater's skater, because her peers appreciate the quality and speed of her skating.

Ruh says she was warmly welcomed to *Stars on Ice*. "It was really positive. The skaters were really wonderful to me. It was always an honor for me to skate on *Stars on Ice* with all the Olympic champions," she reports. "But I think that I really got a lot of respect from the other skaters for what I could do. And I think that everybody could learn from everybody. I think that they also felt that they could learn from what I brought to the ice."

Ruh's success is a bone of contention for many in figure skating.

"It's a little weird [getting all the work she has]," declares Nicole Bobek, a former U.S. Women's Champion and World medalist. "A little odd, because you train your whole life to even be on these tours and at these events, to make accomplishments, so you are invited to participate. It has to do with the whole packaging of a skater. And with someone like Ruh, she has the right agent and the right contacts."

True, Ruh is with the all-powerful IMG, which dictates much of what goes on in pro skating and produces *Stars on Ice*.

But beyond Ruh's connections, there is another reason she—as well as the other gimmick skaters—get hired for work over others with superior credentials. They don't cost as much.

Ruh's salary for *Stars on Ice* was reportedly half of Sato's. With today's unstable economy, everyone in skating is looking to cut corners, resulting in some wonderful skaters getting squeezed out of jobs.

So why did all the work available to skaters, particularly the competitions, vanish so abruptly in 1999 and 2000?

Everyone involved seems to have a different take: television networks stopped paying rights fees, no new skaters entered the pro system; there simply was no pro system anymore and the public got bored with the skaters doing the same programs over and over again. Everybody has something to say, and there's truth to it all.

Understanding the magnitude of the fall is also to appreciate the heights pro skating reached.

"There seemed to be endless possibilities. As a performer, it was hard not to take for granted that there would be six to 12 professional competitions, and, in a way, you were able to pick and choose," recalls Paul Wylie, whose pro career (1992–98) magically paralleled those golden years.

"I opted to maximize whatever I was doing," he adds. "I tried to do the highest quality work, but I also was trying to do as much as possible. There was constant movement and possibility. It was sort of like being in the middle of a tornado. You continue to go, and if someone asks you to do something, you think, *Well I can do it, I can make it, I can fly across the country and get that done.*

"We were very much blessed by that particular time. Yet I think we all worked hard, which caused us to be exhausted at the end of the season. It wasn't like there was so little to go around that people were thinking that there was a lot of jealousy. There was so much going on that you were just trying to do as much as you could, and everybody was doing it."

Brian Orser seconds that. "It was pretty overwhelming how popular figure skating became and how many events there were," he says. "That so many people came to see live events was pretty crazy."

"There were some good events and some bad ones. At the time, though, it seemed like all of them were good," laughs Kristi Yamaguchi. "It was like, *Wow, this is incredible!* I was running around with my head cut off, basically. Looking back, I don't know how I did it.

"A lot of them were fun, like the World Team competition. The one I think that was really neat was the Gold Championships (a competition with only Olympic Champions). It's too bad they don't do those anymore."

Kristi says because of all the pro prospects, she felt like she never lost her competitive edge.

"You know, it felt like I was still competing," she says. "Actually, it was more nuts than eligible competition. Back then we were only two international events a year, plus Nationals and Worlds. Some of the pro events were live TV so you felt like, *Hey, I've got to be ready for this.*"

Looking back at the many events she did, to this day, there is one event that still boggles Kristi's mind.

"The toughest one for me to get through was a show, the Barry Manilow special *(StarSkates Tribute to Barry Manilow)*. I love him. He's great. But that was a tough one for me to swallow," she admits. "I looked at Yuki (Saegusa, her IMG agent) and said, 'How did you let me agree to do this?'"

Kristi, who was at the center of all the action, is actually relieved things have settled down. "It was ridiculous, and I'm actually glad it's not like that anymore. I don't want to have that pressure and think I have to do it again! It was literally going from *Stars on Ice* rehearsals to event, to event, to event," she declares.

Katarina Witt counts her blessings for being at the right place at the right time. "Luckily, we were the generation who was around when a lot of professional competitions were created. It was great for us, because we made a great living," she states.

"It was an unbelievable time. I don't think you realized. You just kind of went from one thing to the next. It wasn't like, *Oh my God, do you realize we are at the peak of the sport?* I don't think it was until now you kind of step back and go, 'Holy mackerel,'" declares Rosalynn Sumners, the 1983 World Women's Champion and 1984 Olympic silver medalist—who readily admits she accepted virtually all events offered to her.

"There were all kinds of professional competitions," notes 1948 and 1952 Olympic Men's Champion Dick Button, whose Candid Productions was responsible for many of these events. "There were many pro competitions, and these pro competitions were doing better television ratings all those years than other sports programming. And it was all because of the Tonya Harding/Nancy Kerrigan fracas."

Then the wheels came off.

"When there was no other scandal or interest from the public, it slipped," states four-time U.S. Women's medalist Caryn Kadavy, who made her share of appearances in the pro and pro/am competitions.

Button doesn't believe that was the case.

"I don't think there was an intense growth of skating there, and I don't think the public lost interest in it," he proclaims. "Everybody is interested in blueberry pie and ice cream, but if you get six pieces of it in the same meal, you're going to get a little sick to your stomach. It doesn't mean that I still don't like blueberry pie and ice cream. I love it."

More precisely, how many times during the mid- to late-1990s did we see the same skater perform the same program, event after event? Pro skating was on overload.

"For us and for everybody, the sport just got saturated," states Rob Correa, senior vice president of programming for CBS Sports, the network that in the mid-1990s was airing six to eight pro competitions per year. "There was too much on with the same people skating the same routines. It's been a marketplace adjustment."

Yet, it was the very networks who dictated which skaters were at events, and the skaters can only produce so many new programs a year.

"The networks were saying, 'We want Nancy Kerrigan, we want Oksana Baiul, we want Katarina Witt,'" says Mike Burg, Tara Lipinski's former agent.

Lack of pride didn't help matters either, notes Button. "Things were just slapped together. Some of the quality was just nonexistent."

Brian Boitano, 1988 Olympic Men's Champion, agrees. "A lot of people are short-sighted. They look at what's going to be best for them at the moment. They look at the response of the crowd. They don't think, *In 10 years, am I going to look back at the video and roll my eyes?*" he contends.

"It's partially the skaters' fault, and it's partially the producers' fault for having some skaters in their shows who don't have any edit buttons. That gives skating a bad name."

While skating was overextending itself, other sports were on the rebound.

Gone were the strikes in hockey and baseball, which had created a crater of opportunity for skating.

"The networks had been looking for events to fill the slots, because they had those strikes. When CBS has a major contract for baseball, and there's a strike, they've got to go find something else. Figure skating seemed to be the next thing that people would tune into at the time," offers Orser.

Skating also flourished because CBS lost the crown jewel in its programming lineup when NFL football went to another network. When the sport returned to CBS, it squeezed out the demand for skating, so the network executives no longer ordered those events for its time slots.

Instead, networks offered the skating competition production companies what is called a "time-buy," where the production companies have to sell sponsorships for the event to pay for the time slot.

Despite skating's decline in popularity, this option may not have been so out of the question if it weren't for the fact that Dick Button sold his Candid Productions company, and the purchaser, SFX Entertainment, subsequently went through a series of mergers. The result was that the people now ultimately responsible for the competitions weren't enthused enough about skating to take the gamble.

Today, there is just one competition on CBS, the team event called Ice Wars, and one head-to-head event on NBC, the Hallmark Skaters' Championships.

"Unfortunately, we don't have Ilia [Kulik] and Kurt [Browning] competing the way we had for a few years Kurt and Brian [Boitano] trying to one up each other," Scott Hamilton says. "That wouldn't have been as exciting if they'd just been putting out these great numbers in a show. It was intense and thrilling because it was in competition."

"With every peak, there's going to be a valley," says a philosophical Kurt Browning. "I don't think anyone is surprised it's dropped off a bit. It's not like, *What have I done wrong?* It's just a cycle."

Kurt believes the past success, and today's lack thereof, can be traced to the skaters themselves.

"We had fantastic personalities for a while—fantastic North American stars. Now Russians have eclipsed them. We have Russians seemingly winning everything, and what that's doing is that we're not recreating those North American stars, which is where the market is. That's just a fact," he explains.

"If Todd Eldredge had won the [2002] Olympics—being an American and with his history of staying eligible and coming back for one last shot—boom, instant hero. Alexei Yagudin (the Olympic

Men's gold medalist, from Russia) is not. That's one of the things that have been hard lately, and I don't think it's a bad thing to say.

"Michelle Kwan has been fantastic for the sport of figure skating, but she's stayed eligible for eight years and so have most of the others. The professional ranks are not being infused with new stars, huge stars," Browning adds. "Another example is, Tara Lipinski turned pro before her amateur career gave her a chance to be really well-known."

As a result, Tara has not enjoyed the pinnacle of popularity enjoyed by Michelle Kwan or Kristi Yamaguchi. And of the only four or five skaters of any note who have turned pro since the 1998 Nagano Olympics, Tara was the most visible.

"We just really haven't had what we had eight years ago when I was with Paul Wylie, Brian Boitano and Brian Orser. All of these people sort of turned pro together. Also Kristi Yamaguchi. It was a very exciting time. Plus, we had Nancy and Tonya and two Olympics in four years. That certainly helped," Browning surmises.

"The ranks of pro skating have been depleted," determines Byron Allen, vice president of Winter Sports at IMG. "After the 1998 Winter Games, a key piece to the puzzle, the key North American male, didn't turn pro. That would be Todd Eldredge. Neither did Elvis Stojko."

While both of these elder statesmen have realistically closed the door on future Olympic-style competitions, it may be too late to help pro skating. Plus, their careers aren't quite at the heights they were four years ago.

Then there is Eldredge's remarkable desire to maintain his eligibility and his preference for the International Skating Union (ISU) open format competitions, commonly called pro/ams, where both professional and Olympic-eligible skaters participate.

"Hopefully, the ISU will make that into its own type of series," Eldredge suggests. ISU President Ottavio Cinquanta has already publicly talked about this possibility.

The pro/ams came about due to the USFSA and ISU's desire to keep its skaters Olympic-eligible, yet allow them to compete in a more relaxed environment—and more importantly, to horn in on the success pro skating was experiencing.

Some established professionals—such as Browning—have enjoyed participating in the pro/ams, while others view them as part of the problem.

"I love them. I think they're great for skating," proclaims Brian Orser. "They are great for the seasoned pros, because when you are competing against Alexei Yagudin or Todd Eldredge, you have to work extra hard. They challenge us in the technical program, and we challenge them in the artistic or interpretive program. So, ultimately, skating as a whole goes up to another level."

"As a bonus, the pro/am events are ISU judged. And to be honest, they're not as crooked as the pro competitions. On the whole, the pro/ams have always been fairer."

On the other side is Brian Boitano.

"The pro/ams really hurt the sport. It was a big mistake adding the amateurs. It really decreased the popularity of the World Professional Figure Skating Championships, in particular, and it made it not as serious," he declares.

"That was a serious event, and then, all of a sudden, to bring amateurs in and have a whole different style of judging. And those skaters honestly didn't care if they won it or not—it wasn't to them an important title. It was the beginning of the end for World Pro."

What does the event's creator, Dick Button, think?

"I had a long feeling about the professional world and the amateur world that they should be separated. Then at one point, I began to feel that they could be combined. Then I very quickly realized that no, they can't be combined, and they shouldn't be combined," shares Button.

Button's prevailing thought, however, had been that he always wanted the World Pro to have the best skaters in the world competing, whether they be pro or eligible, states former Candid Productions associate producer Craig Cichy. But in the end, Button didn't like the co-mingling of the two groups at the 1998 competition, and eligible skaters were not included in the event the following year.

"Each represents different aspects of thought, as to the approach. I think what made the professional world successful was that it maintained both the very difficult technical merit of skating, but it brought into equal emphasis the creative, sensitive, artistic side of the sport," determines Button.

Cichy says it was an added burden on the Candid Productions staff the year the welcome mat was rolled out for the eligible skaters.

"It was hard, because we were working with an additional group that we hadn't really needed to work with before and trying to fit what we have always been doing into a new regimen of sorts," he says. "Because the ISU and the USFSA were involved, we had to do things a certain way that we had not had to do before. For example, we had to have dope testers there, and the skaters had to be tested for doping, which we had never done in pro skating, and we had to have certain accountants tabulating and verifying results. Certain procedures had to be followed.

"We had put together these events, and we had been working on travel, logistics and the sponsor and everything that goes into putting an event together, and, all of a sudden, there is a hammer thrown in the wheel, and we have to change everything.

"One ridiculous thing the USFSA/ISU made us do was to change the name of the event, because evidently the ISU has a rule that says you can't use the word 'championships,' which means the World Professional Figure Skating Championships couldn't be called that."

But that notification came too late to change some materials, much to the chagrin of ISU Council Member Claire Ferguson. She marched into the pressroom and told publicity director Lynn Plage to yank down the banner, which used "championships" in the title.

"That banner had already been made by our sponsor, and there was no way to change it, because it had already been made when we found out that we couldn't use the word 'championships.' Also, we had to protect our own trademark of that title—to consistently keep using it so you don't lose the trademark that we had on the event," Cichy explains. "So in some printed materials and on the awards and in a lot of the pre-event press materials, the full title, the trademark title, was used.

"I know that there was a lot of disgust with that press banner and some of the other materials that we were having posted around the arena, like the skate order. And we had our logo on there, and we had the full title on it and just things like that that the ISU didn't want up, but I didn't understand the big deal about it, because if the ISU was so happy to be involved with this event, then call it a championship. Because that is what it was."

The real fun, says Cichy, came before the events ever took place, when Candid Productions didn't even know if the ISU or USFSA were going to sanction one of the pro competitions, thus allowing eligible skaters to participate, and Candid Productions was expected to continue with plans.

"It was really frustrating that year, because by the time we actually had an event scheduled and we were starting to work on it—I don't remember what the circumstances were, but all of a sudden we would hear, 'They are not going to sanction it,' which would mean we have no event," Cichy states.

"We had promised the network certain skaters, and blah, blah, and now, because it wasn't sanctioned, that was going to kill the event. I mean, a couple of the events were yanked only days before they were to happen. It was really an awful year!"

In the final analysis, Button feels the USFSA doesn't understand how to make the pro/am events work. "That's why they've not been wildly successful programs, even though I narrate them," admits Button, who is also a veteran television commentator. "I think some of the competitions are confused, unfocused and don't really have a point of view. But that's all right. That's all part of the growing pains."

There was another force working against pro skating. When pro competitions were in their prime, the ISU, skating's top governing body, decided to take its own action to keep a hold on the best eligible skaters—so it, not the pro world, would be the one reaping the rewards from television and sponsors.

With the 1995–96 season, the Grand Prix series was born, in which skaters earn prize money based on placement at each of the six international competitions and the series final. This advent erased the notion that turning pro was the only way for a skater to continue his or her craft and make a good living.

The result is that very few skaters have since entered the pro arena, a sore spot for many veteran performers.

"Sometimes it now seems like skaters are making a business decision, because if they look out, what is in the pro world? Damn, if I'm not going to get on *Stars on Ice*, then how am I going to earn a living? But I know if I keep competing, and I do OK, and I'm in the top 10 in the world, I know I can go to the Grand Prix events and earn prize money," says Scott Hamilton.

"Many skaters think if they don't have an Olympic or a World medal or an invitation to join one of the two top tours, they might as well stay competing. What they're actually doing is selling themselves short.

"When you're competing on the eligible level, you get to have a medal hung around your neck every year to tell you how good you are. When you're a professional, it comes down to you evaluating yourself and to have an audience tell you if they approve of what you're doing or not. That's pure."

What is of the utmost concern to Scott is the advice today's eligible skaters are getting on their careers and the domino effect that has on the pro world he was so intimately involved in establishing.

"It worries me, because I feel like professional skating right now is going to suffer because of the images that are being put forth by the people who have access to these young competitive skaters right now. 'No, you don't want to do that right now, you want to stay here, you want to be where it's safe and where you can make all this money,'" he contends.

"In effect, what they're not telling skaters is that, yes, it's nice and safe here [in eligible skating] and here's your bird in the hand—only they are not letting them know there are two birds in the bush, if they'll only go looking in pro skating.

"What this genre gives to the people who love to watch beautiful movement is that it is like a great art of dance on many different levels and many different styles. But it's accelerated, and it's athletic in its nature. I feel a lot of skaters get in touch with who they are as skaters once they step away from the competitive stage and have to stand on their own."

One who did is the 1998 Olympic Men's Champion Ilia Kulik, who immediately left the eligible ranks behind after that triumph. He says he believes that money isn't a deciding factor in a skater's decision to stay or leave the eligible circuit.

"The two types of skating are so different; I don't think it is money that only decides. It's more if you want to skate a different way, if you want to work on different things. If you want to work more on difficulty or the technical side, you stay amateur. If you want to open up a little more artistically and spend your year doing shows and entertaining people, that's the pro way of life," Ilia explains.

"Probably, now, money-wise, it's close to the same," he continues. "I'm not sure though. It's totally different work to do, and that's how you choose. It's like different professions; you are choosing a different way of living, different way of working and different things to work on."

Brian Boitano believes the paying of eligible skaters may become a moot point. "I know maybe I'm the only person to really think it's going to change, but I don't think an older skater is going to want to stay in [eligible competitions] if they start losing—especially one who has some sort of reputation," he states. "There's got to be a certain point where the skaters will say no to the money, because they don't really want to compete at that level anymore. I think they'll jump ship."

But what will they jump ship to? Not every eligible skater who enjoyed some degree of success will end up on a major tour like *Stars on Ice* or *Champions on Ice*. Only two competitions and seven exhibition shows receive television coverage. What is a pro skater to do?

"You have to be flexible. You have to be willing to do things that may not be quite as comfortable as they used to be," offers Jozef Sabovcik, the 1984 Olympic Men's bronze medalist, whose pro career took off thanks to the television exposure he received in pro competitions in the 1990s.

A case in point: several times last season, Jozef flew to Japan to perform.

"You have to go with the flow," he says. "I really do like to skate and perform. It has its drawbacks. I'm not with my family as much. That's something you have to take into account. This kind of work will not last forever for me. As long as I still have fun doing what I'm doing, I want to keep doing it."

Eric Millot, the former French Champion and Olympic and World competitor, has also felt the scarcity of events.

"The last two years, there are less jobs on the market. When I see other skaters performing, I think, *I could be one of these skaters in this tour or that show*," he contends. "It's very important to have the opportunity to skate as much as you can. Because producers forget you. If nobody pushes you, you stay on the side and you stay home!"

To help remedy that dilemma for himself and other skaters, Eric has decided to become an agent. He is working with adagio (theatrical) pair skaters Anita Hartshorn & Frank Sweiding, who have their own production company, Glacier Ice. They are adding a representation division, which Eric will run.

"There are a lot of skaters who don't have representation," Eric says. "There is work out there. They need someone to help them find it."

"Sometimes it's hard to keep practicing, because you wonder, *Gosh, am I even going to have a show coming up?*" says former U.S. medalist Tonia Kwiatkowski. "You may have nothing planned, but you always have to be prepared. I truly love to skate. It's hard when I don't have anything coming up for a while."

Kwiatkowski's most substantial job last season was a month-long run in *Footloose on Ice*, a show produced by Nancy Kerrigan at the Ice Castle Theatre in Myrtle Beach, S.C.

Two-time Olympic bronze medalist Philippe Candeloro reasons, "I've done well professionally, because I have a name. Some skaters don't have any name. It's difficult for me to tell them to turn pro, because they may not have any work to do."

Candeloro, like Nancy Kerrigan with her stage shows and Elvis Stojko with his Canadian tour, has done his best to generate opportunities.

"I created my own tour in France," Candeloro says. "I offer skaters work. Some people want as much as is paid in America, but that's impossible, especially with the small buildings we sometimes play. Some skaters understand and some don't."

The reality is there are a lot of jobs to be had—just not jobs as glamorous as those available during the skating boom.

"I'm here to say, there's plenty of work," declares Jeb Rand, president of Rand Enterprises and Productions, as well as an adagio pair skater with partner-wife Jennifer Bayer. "Some skaters are looking for the perfect job. The bubble burst a few years ago, in my opinion. The professional skaters have to be a little more open-minded and be willing to try new things and understand that one contract might pay X, but the next contract might pay twice X. They're going to have to be willing to try things."

Dan Hollander, former U.S. medalist, concurs. "It just depends on how hungry you are and what's the niche you can offer," he says. "I've got this Santa Claus gig that I do in Texas all the time. They fly me out, and I'm the Skating Santa Claus. It can be done. You can make a living."

Hollander also is one of the lucky ones. Besides his willingness to do small-scale jobs, he's been on the *Champions on Ice* tour for the past three years, thanks to his own gimmick routines, which are high in comedy and low in technical content.

Hollander got on this top tour through perseverance and not being afraid to have to prove himself to its producer, Tom Collins.

"As my competitive career wound down, I was getting less and less work. Finally, I came up with my old lady routine, where I go from *South Park* to *Mrs. Doubtfire*. I called my agent at the time, Michael Rosenberg, and said, 'Call up Tom Collins and tell him I just want to show him this number in Detroit (when the tour stopped there).' I showed it to him, and the following year he asked me to come on full time," explains Dan.

The other gimmick skaters in *Champions on Ice*, The Acrobats and The Hula-Hoop Girl, also had screen tests before they were given jobs. For his part, Dan sees them as variety acts and considers himself "a single skater who adds in comedy." In truth, he does get off a triple toe jump now and again, but his programs are more hamming it up with the audience than anything else.

Dan sees going for the laughs as a trend of sorts. "You have [Olympic Champion] Viktor Petrenko skating with a doll, [World Champion] Evgeni Plushenko in the muscle man outfit last year and [two-time Olympic bronze medalists] Isabelle Brasseur & Lloyd Eisler have their switched-sex routine. A lot of skaters are realizing that comedy is a great way to go," he states. "It gets a fantastic response with the crowds."

If you can't carve a niche for yourself like Hollander, but want steady work, there are two touring productions that provide skaters a lot of opportunities for a career, even if the notoriety is non-existent.

Kenneth Feld, the president and CEO of Feld Entertainment, has the most available jobs for figure skaters via his global *Disney on Ice* tours. The skaters in *Disney* perform in 10 to 12 story-based shows a week. Though the skaters won't make it on television, and the pay is far less than the superstar-driven tours, these are good, steady jobs.

In 1979, Feld bought the North American segment of the *Holiday on Ice* touring show, shut it down and started a show with an entirely new look—one based on the Disney tales. While everybody in skating talks about bringing in the younger demographic, Feld actually went out and captured it, by creating a tour that was pure family entertainment.

"In the latter part of '80, I went to Disney, and I went there with the intention of trying to get a 20-minute sort of production number within the show using Disney characters and themes. And Disney rejected the idea," shares Feld. "As I was leaving the office, I said, 'What happens if we convert one of our ice shows to all Disney characters and themes and we call it *Walt Disney's World on Ice?*' That's the genesis."

Though it was hardly smooth sailing. "The first *Walt Disney's World on Ice* show was in July of 1981, and the arenas and the media were so skeptical that I actually had to guarantee the same amount of business that we had done the prior year with *Ice Follies* or *Holiday on Ice* to a lot of the major arenas, in order to get the dates in there," reveals Feld.

"Of course, the business that we did that first year was incredible," he continues. "We grew it, and the following year we had a second show, and then 1986 was the first year that we went international. Now we are up to eight different *Disney* shows around the world."

So who are the skaters who typically work for Feld? "I retain a high level of integrity with the skating, but I don't need Olympic or World medalists to do that," states Feld. "What I do need are world class skaters like Craig Heath (a U.S. National competitor, but never a medalist), who was with us for six years starring in *Toy Story*."

Craig believes skaters who could be working as he does shy away from it, because of the gypsy lifestyle.

"People are afraid of traveling so much," he theorizes. "Yet once you get into the rhythm of traveling with a show like *Holiday on Ice* or *Disney on Ice*, where you're traveling constantly for a long time, it's really fun. We're not just in a city for a night. We're in a city for a week, sometimes two weeks, sometimes three. We get to relax and to have different experiences all the time. It's pretty incredible to say, 'Oh, I'm in Paris for two weeks.'"

Feld says his casting director travels month in, month out searching for skaters with Craig's willingness and understanding of the demands of the tour, which sometimes includes performing a six-pack: three shows a day for two days. Feld also looks for "specific types and characters and people to play certain roles."

He avows unabashed respect for Craig and his drive to sustain his technical abilities—even in an elaborate costume.

"Sometimes at the end of the show, he would come out and perform a series of double axels for the audience," recalls Feld.

But what if being a Disney character doesn't float a skater's boat?

Skaters can pack their bags for Europe and join one of the five shows under the *Holiday on Ice* umbrella, owned by Stageholding and run by CEO Eric-Paul Dijkhuizen of the Netherlands. Over the last few years, *Holiday on Ice* has brought in renowned choreographer and 1980 Olympic Men's Champion Robin Cousins to revamp the show. They have endeavored to use more contemporary music and themes, as well as state-of-the-art lighting and sound systems.

Holiday is quite unique in that it aims to satisfy customers from vastly different countries with a similar product. The tour has the most stops in Germany, but plays throughout Europe, so they must be cognizant that what might go over well in Germany may not be such a hit in France or England. They have to find a way to transcend national bias.

"There is a big danger that you get towards the German market too much or that you just focus too much on what your own background is and gear it toward [in my case] more Dutch, more artsy kind of direction," admits Dijkhuizen. "So what I try to do is take cultural elements from time to time that go across the globe, because it is a global blend that we are stirring, and the taste has to be good. It has to be appreciated.

"There are possibilities in our show that we can highlight certain elements a bit more by adding—for example, in France we did add some local performers, and we did change some of the music, so there are some other things we can adapt in our shows," he adds.

To handle the business or marketing side of having a tour in various countries, Dijkhuizen says *Holiday* maintains several regional offices, including ones in Germany, England and The Netherlands.

"It would be very wrong to assume we can rule the world from Amsterdam. You don't know how an American looks at a theme park versus a European. Same thing for ice shows. You have to work with local marketing people," he states.

Dijkhuizen believes the technology innovations currently in *Holiday* would be a great lure for American audiences and is currently exploring options to bring one of the tours, *Colours of Dance*, to North America in 2003. As Feld owns the *Holiday on Ice* name in North America, they will have to find another title for the tour.

What is pro skating's future? Will there be a resurgence? It's hard to say at this point. Some, like *Stars on Ice* choreographer Sandra Bezic, believe it's possible. "It's the personalities. If you get somebody who captures the imagination of the public, then pro skating will revive," she claims.

Others don't believe things are so simple and aren't as optimistic.

"Through the whole cycle of all the events skating had, the only one that's left standing [from the boom period] for the moment is Ice Wars. I think the demise of pro competition demonstrates one of the greatest missed opportunities in the history of sports. Not skating—in the history of sports," declares sports executive Jerry Solomon, who is also the husband and manager of Nancy Kerrigan.

"I've lived through some of the great debates in tennis and other sports, and never have I seen, given what was at stake, parties involved that would be so unable to come to a meeting of the minds as what has taken place in skating," he continues. "It's all because of their own shortsightedness and selfishness."

"Everybody wanted to control the whole pie," admits Mike Burg, the force behind Ice Wars and formerly of Jefferson Pilot Sports, one company that was battling the giant IMG over CBS television spots, skaters and domination.

The ultimate result of such power plays was that no one benefited.

"What should be today a worldwide pro circuit, a worldwide skating circuit, involving Olympic and non-Olympic eligible skaters, what should be in place today is not even close to being in place. So you see figure skating, the TV numbers, sponsorships and opportunities dropping off the face of the earth," Solomon states.

Scott Hamilton hasn't liked what he's seen either.

"A lot of people who don't know anything about pro skating are currently making the decisions for it," he declares.

"Whether it's people who say, 'Well, our research shows that our audience for these competitions are 15 percent more than they are for exhibitions.' I don't know about that. I think that it's a lot of guys in the sports departments who are used to selling beer in trucks that don't really understand the intricacies of skating and the audience that you can have there.

"All that stuff gets really trendy. The kind of philosophy in sports television as far as skating is concerned is, *What do you think?* It's not done on what's real, it's done on what somebody feels it is. That has to change!"

It Was All for the Federation

"All those who want to be involved do it because they want to prove they can do it better. This is the motivation. In business, arts and sports, when one stands and says, 'I would like to be involved,' it means he or she believes he or she can do it better than the others."

– Ottavio Cinquanta, President
International Skating Union

It Was All for the Federation

S ome of the most powerful jobs in the sport of figure skating are unpaid.

Those individuals who govern all eligible aspects of the sport—from the International Skating Union (ISU), the international sports federation that oversees all of skating, to the national federations—are all volunteers.

Some of these volunteers are independently wealthy, some are retired and some simply find a way to balance the demands of their unpaid career with their regular jobs.

Do they do it for the love of the sport or for the power? Both.

"The volunteer aspect of our federation is what separates us from a for-profit corporation and being a big business," notes Phyllis Howard, president of the United States Figure Skating Association (USFSA) and newly elected member of the ISU Council. "People are very passionate about their involvement in skating. Most of the time, it's been a life-time involvement in this sport. We must never forget that."

Some people were skaters themselves. That would be the case for most of the judges. Some had children who skated. Long after the children had moved on to other pursuits, the parents remained entrenched in the sport.

"There is an attraction to it. I think it's a disease," Howard jokes. "There is an opportunity in this sport to be more than just a parent. There is a chance for people to be involved in meaningful ways—whether it's as an accountant at a competition or an announcer at a competition, helping to raise money at a local club or getting into the judging ranks."

"This service bit is BS," says John LeFevre, now executive director of the USFSA (a paid position), but until 1998, a lifelong volunteer. "I used to get so mad, because some people would say it was the morally right thing to do. I said, 'You do this because it makes you feel good. You get all those strokes from it.' It was true, and it is still true to a certain extent today.

"I did not realize how many people pander to judges, until I stopped being a judge," he continues. "Then I thought, *Gee, I am just another one of the peons.* When I was a judge, I had no idea how many people viewed judges as some sort of exotic race or something. It seemed like everybody sort of sucks up to them."

On the international level, judges travel by business class, not coach, and they stay at five-star hotels. They also wield power to make life-changing decisions.

Volunteers who perform other functions—ranging from registration, to accounting, to various administrative details—experience a wide range of treatment: from being exalted to being ignored.

LeFevre says he saw a shift in the volunteer base in the early 1990s, when people tended to become more business savvy. Regardless of their backgrounds, the USFSA, other national skating associations and the ISU remain organizations run by unpaid workers, who often times have their own agendas—some public and some hidden.

LeFevre says many USFSA volunteers resented the hiring of Jerry Lace, a savvy sports administrator who became the association's executive director, in the early 1990s. "He was an outsider," LeFevre notes. But as they saw the financial fortunes of the association rising and money being channeled into a wide variety of programs, Lace ultimately became a well respected individual.

"What he did was bring the USFSA into the 20th century from a business standpoint, which we needed to be, because, essentially, a lot of what was going on was done by well meaning volunteers who really didn't know what was going on in the business world then," he says.

Balancing the desires of a volunteer corps and the business needs of the organization is an ongoing process. The bottom line is that the volunteers are essential to carry out the myriad of jobs. Some volunteers have enormous talents and are capable of making great contributions at a very high level. All are principally driven by a love of the sport.

One thing national associations have had to come to terms with is that, now, skaters earn their livelihood from the sport while continuing to compete. For most skaters, that means earning prize money, coaching and skating in the occasional show. For top skaters, like Michelle Kwan and Elvis Stojko, it means big business—from tours, to TV specials, to huge endorsement deals, some of which may conflict with the corporate sponsors supporting the association.

"Skate Canada is really great, but it's never going to be hunky-dory perfect," says Stojko. "No family is perfect, no organization is perfect, but if you're open to communication and you don't take things aggressively, you'll be OK. Sometimes people get upset, and boom, boom, boom, you get in trouble. You just have to play it smart. You have to be able to have common sense. You have to be able to work with people, and that is what a good organization does."

Stojko says he understands that Skate Canada needs to raise funds and promote itself, and sometimes it must push boundaries to accomplish its objectives. He then turns to his attorney/business manager, Ed Futerman, to advocate in his best interests.

Some skaters try to take part in their associations, and some admit to little or no knowledge.

"I didn't pay much attention to the USFSA," says three-time U.S. Women's Champion Rosalynn Sumners. "I was just sort of in my little world. It was like, 'OK, let's go to the Olympics.' Then I turned pro.

"It is not like a Michelle Kwan, who stayed in for quite a few years, where you really are using the support of the USFSA."

Some skaters look to their associations for funding. Some simply look for their national federations to promote their names when they go to compete internationally.

"The Russian federation and the Eastern bloc countries work the system," asserts 1992 Olympic Pair silver medalist Elena Bechke, from Russia, who now lives and coaches in Virginia. "These people are just more pushy. I think North Americans don't do it because it's just not them, not their style.

"I've heard a lot of stories about Russian coaches and federation members approaching judges. It's because the Russian federation has so much power. It keeps happening and becomes habit."

Judges are supposed to judge fairly and impartially. They take an oath to that effect at the Olympic Opening Ceremonies. But in skating, everyone expects there is a certain amount of lobbying for good favor.

Even Didier Gailhaguet, president of the Federation Française des Sports de Glace (French skating federation), who denies pressuring French judge Marie-Reine Le Gougne to favor the Russian pair team in the 2002 Olympics, readily admits he lobbied judges and officials in favor of French skaters.

It is the job of referees to report all such pressure, be it brazen or subtle, to the Technical Committees. But all too often, that simply doesn't happen.

"The European referees are not receptive to efforts to report these incidents," notes Benjamin Wright, who became a judge in 1942. Wright was an ISU championship judge and referee in both figure skating and ice dancing. He was involved with six Olympics and 25 World Championships as either a judge or referee, retiring 10 years ago by mandate at age 70. He also served on the ISU Figure Skating Technical Committee for 19 years, including four years as chairman.

"There are all kinds of intimidation," Wright explains. "One is the country, the little country, which has a skater. They come to the big country that has a skater at the top. The little country says to a big country judge, 'If you don't mark my skater, who is 17th, up to 15th, then I am going to take your skater from first to third.' That would be the intimidation approach. I have seen that. The other type, of course, is, 'If you will do this for me, I do that for you.'"

Skaters have come to expect their national federations to be doing such work on their behalf.

"I didn't have an influential force working for me, which I should have," says Brian Orser, two-time Olympic Men's silver medalist from Canada. "If only a little lobbying on my behalf had taken place.

"Canada just doesn't always do enough."

Not so, says one former Canadian judge who spoke on the condition of anonymity.

"Canada has been noted for pressuring its judges, and I spoke out about it in a meeting we had, called Skating in Transition. I said, 'I don't want to see it continued. It is wrong. When we are in Europe, we are judging as an international skating judge. We are not representing a country.' Another championship judge stood up and noted that Canada is being chastised for this sort of thing," recalls the judge.

When the minutes of the meeting were printed and distributed, the comments were not included in the record.

"Whenever they can't control someone, they move them out of the way," says the judge.

This appears to be the case of Canadian Ann Shaw, who has been on the ISU Ice Dance Technical Committee since 1992.

When Wolfgang Kunz, chairman of the Ice Dance Technical Committee from 1996–98, opted not to run for re-election at the 1998 Congress, Shaw decided to run for the spot.

"On the eve of the election, Betty Bouma, who was then president of the Canadian Figure Skating Association (now renamed Skate Canada), came to me and said, 'We are not going to propose you for chair,'" Shaw says. "I think it had to do with an agreement with other countries to have a Russian chair. So on the eve of the election, she said, 'I am not supporting you.' It was like being hit by a lead balloon. I went to her the next morning, after having discussed it with my husband, and said, 'If you are not supporting me for my running for chair, I am not running for the Committee,' and they wanted me on the Committee. About five minutes later, they came back and said they were going to drop the Russian alliance and are going to support me for the chair."

Shaw was defeated in her bid for chairwoman, but easily won re-election to the Committee. Her disappointment with the events in 1998 would be exceeded by what transpired prior to and during the 2002 ISU Congress in Kyoto, Japan.

Shortly before the Congress, Skate Canada announced its list of candidates for ISU offices. Shaw was not among those named. Rather, Skate Canada was supporting Jack Greenwood in a bid for a spot on the Ice Dance Technical Committee.

"When they proposed Jack, it really meant that they were proposing him to run against me," says Shaw, who received the news from Skate Canada president Marilyn Chidlow. "I was not backing down. I think they may have expected that I would back down at that point, but I did not.

"I felt like I was hit with a board with a nail in the end."

Shaw says Chidlow offered little explanation. "Except that it is in the interest of our skaters and skating," she says.

A call to Chidlow to comment on this issue for *Frozen Assets* was not returned.

"Jack Greenwood is a very, very ambitious man," says the unnamed former judge.

At the Congress in Kyoto, when it became clear Greenwood didn't have the international support to be elected to the Committee, but Shaw did, Skate Canada withdrew his name. But that was by no means an enthusiastic support of Shaw. When Shaw decided to run for chairwoman, Chidlow stood up and made a speech endorsing Shaw's opponent, Alexander Gorshkov.

Gorshkov won the election for chairman, and Shaw was re-elected to the Committee for another four years. She says she wonders what she did to offend Skate Canada, but also says she still has a passion for the sport and won't abandon it. As both she and her husband are retired—she as a teacher and he as executive vice president of Nestle Canada—she has the time to do the job. She is mindful that there isn't a surplus of eager, young judges and officials waiting to step to the fore when she's ready to leave skating.

ISU President Cinquanta is abundantly aware of this dilemma.

"My task now is to prepare new managers, new administrators for the future," he says. "There is a certain lack of enthusiasm among the young."

Cinquanta insists it is not impossible to balance a career with high-level involvement with skating.

"With an efficient administration, it is possible," he says. "You cannot do everything alone."

But Sally Stapleford, from Great Britain, who served as chairwoman of the ISU Figure Skating Technical Committee (overseeing the judges and referees for singles and pair skating) from 1992–2002 (when she was defeated at the Congress by Alexander Lakernik of Russia), says the ISU provided no such administration.

"The chairperson's role is a full time job, as I was away for many months a year acting as a referee, running seminars and judges' exams, attending numerous meetings, etc.," she recounts. "Then, when I was home, I would be in my office from early in the morning until late at night doing all the necessary paperwork, which was very frustrating, as I felt like a secretary. I was of the view that my talents were not really being used to their best advantage, as I was being bogged down in paperwork without a secretary to assist me."

It wasn't all negative. In addition to the travel and solicitous treatment, Stapleford got to direct judges, referees and coaches around the world on aspects of skating, thus advancing the development of the sport. She got to be integrally involved in something she loved, and she got to wield a great deal of power—over judges and officials.

There is also power over the results. Judges decide who wins and who doesn't.

"Like any coach in a dressing room before an event starts, the referee reminds the judges of the rules and what they provide for and what they are supposed to do," says Wright. "The rules are spelled out, and they have to judge what they see."

But Cinquanta is mindful that doesn't always happen. In the wake of the judging scandal that rocked the Olympics in Salt Lake City, he has made radical proposals, including a new judging system.

"The new judging system could give to television endless possibilities," Cinquanta says. "People can follow the event much better."

But there is one crucial factor—Cinquanta, who was elected ISU president in 1994, was never a figure skater. The ISU is comprised of representatives from figure skating (including ice dancing), speed skating and short track speed skating. Cinquanta was a short track speed skater. His first ISU post was as a member of the Short Track Technical Committee.

"The sport is led by a speed skater–president who, in my opinion, showed the world arrogance, unpleasantness, expeditiousness and a quick-fix personality," expounds former agent and producer Michael Rosenberg.

While those involved in the administration of the sport speak of Cinquanta in much more positive and respectful tones, several do refer to his dictatorial style.

"Ottavio does like to be the spokesperson," notes one official. "In a corporation, the CEO usually deals with the media.

"But he is not a judge, and he is not a figure skater. I don't think he quite understands all the facets of certain situations. He is an autocratic, European-type CEO."

"Mr. Cinquanta has great charisma and obviously has a good financial brain; these qualities and others are necessary in any president, whether coming from figure skating or speed skating," says Stapleford. "The obvious difference, if a figure skater was the president, is that this person might naturally have far more understanding of figure skating from day one. There is a reason to have separate vice presidents for figure skating and speed skating, and they need to have authority which recognizes that."

In a 1998 interview, Cinquanta told *International Figure Skating*, "Diplomacy and democracy should not be confused with superficiality. It is very easy to appear [democratic]. You run the Council meeting, you say nothing. This is not diplomacy. This is not democracy. This is just somebody, he's a lazy guy, a person who doesn't want to take care about certain problems. You have to face the problems."

By not allowing the judges and referees to answer the questions of the media, Cinquanta, at times, leaves it open for less informed parties to expound on their opinions.

"There are many inaccuracies in the press," says Shaw. "I hesitate to say too much to the press, because if I find an inaccuracy, it sounds like someone in the ISU is trying to stifle me."

Cinquanta's actions are based on the old time ISU rules.

"Won't do it," responds Wright, when asked to comment on if he ever suspected bloc judging or other judging improprieties occurred at an event at which he officiated. "I live by the rules of the ISU which apply to me, and those rules prohibit officials from commenting on events at which they officiated. So, while I did six Olympic Games and 25 World Championships as a judge and referee, I don't consider it appropriate for me to comment on those.

"I am disturbed by the fact that these judges all now seem to be commenting all over the place, and they are not supposed to do that. The prerogative of commenting is that of the committees and the Council, and I think it is very dangerous for these judges to be talking off-the-cuff the way they have been doing ever since Salt Lake City."

At the Congress in Kyoto, Cinquanta set plans in motion to investigate a restructuring of the ISU. To date, he has declined to detail the nature of that restructuring.

Stapleford says, "I think that most of the structure should be professionalized, to make sure that you employ the very best people for the job, who can be hired and fired."

But who would do the hiring and firing cannot easily be defined. In the end, that would likely be a volunteer, who is doing it all for the federation.

"Only people without good vision could jeopardize or limit the important value of the ISU," says Cinquanta. "We have the two most important activities in the world of entertainment—music and sport. We have both. We want to present this at the highest level.

"The strength of the ISU is that we have a certain style," he adds.

"The president has protected his federation."

Pressures, Perks and Paydays

8

"This generation feels like they are sort of above everything that it took all of us to create in the sport and to get it to where it is today. I think a lot of the skaters simply don't know or care who opened the doors or how they got opened."

– Rosalynn Sumners, 1983 World Women's Champion, 1984 Olympic silver medalist

Pressures, Perks and Paydays

Within the past decade, eligible skating has hit the big time.

Since the 1995–96 season, skaters shining in this arena have earned paychecks for competing in their sport.

They've also tasted fame, courtesy of the media's soaring interest in figure skating.

The sport's technical demands have increased by leaps and bounds, with pressure put on the men to land quadruple jumps and on the women to do triple-triple jump combinations.

How have these changes shaped skaters and impacted their career ambitions?

Before the mid-1990s, the sport's brightest stars turned professional at a relatively young age, because there was no real money to be made in the amateur ranks. Now we see skaters competing in the Olympics at age 30 and driving Ferraris.

"There are so many phenomenal eligible skaters out there right now. So many athletes doing things that have never been done before—just so much talent and so much ability. But there's a mentality that's different now. I'm not saying it's worse, it's just different. The skaters are millionaires when they're competing, and there's a lot of pressure on them to do a lot of other things," says Scott Hamilton.

They're no longer called amateur—the official designation is eligible. But people rarely use that. In fact, in 2002, Michelle Kwan was honored by the Amateur Athletic Union with their Sullivan Award, for being the nation's top amateur athlete.

"I laugh at it when they call it competition. It's a joke. If athletes are going to receive money at Nationals and at Worlds, I don't consider that being an amateur. Just call it entertainment. It's big business. You shouldn't call it amateur anymore, because it's not," declares 1979 World Pair Champion Tai Babilonia.

"I mention what so-and-so got paid, and people are shocked when they hear that. It's like, don't feel too sorry for these skaters, because they are doing OK."

Offering another perspective is 1998 Olympic Men's gold medalist Ilia Kulik, who believes the influx of money has helped skaters focus on the task at hand and not on how they're going to stretch their funds.

"It makes their preparation each season so much easier. You can invest more money in your routine, you can rest well, you can eat well, you have a practice base where you want to have it and, overall, be a little more comfortable. All of which really gives you more energy to practice and will move the skating forward," he states.

"That's definitely the great side about it. You are able to be more independent, also, as you're preparing for the season, so you can really work as you want to work—not to be dependent on anything or anyone."

Babilonia's partner, Randy Gardner, backs Kulik on that point.

"Letting them make money is good in a lot of ways, in that they can support their skating, they can support their training and coaches can make money off of it, too," he says.

But he also believes there is a downside. "Skaters don't compete for the love of the sport. Instead, it's, 'Should I take this international competition, because it's this amount of money if I'm in the top three, or should I not?' So what happens is they wind up doing certain things for the money, and it's almost like they only train hard if there is money in the end of it."

On the same page is Brian Orser, "These eligible skaters won't do anything without asking, 'How much? What's in it for me?'"

And, if you're a major American star, the amount could be quite a tidy sum. Chances are, you are getting an appearance fee to grace the competition with your presence—regardless of where you finish.

The fees, which have gone as high as into six figures, are something Brian Boitano believes will eventually come to an end.

"It's going to be tough for the ISU and USFSA (via the deals with TV networks) to keep doing this, because of the type of money skaters are asking [to appear]," he says. "These are salaries like the professionals are making. Professional skaters used to make that when they could sell a TV show from their names. An amateur skater might be famous in the world of figure skating, but to sell a project, most are not really well known to the public.

"The ISU and USFSA are going to end up paying a lot more than they ever imagined that they would to keep people in amateur skating. But at the same time, they are not necessarily going to be the most famous people. So they are going to end up forking over a lot of money for someone who might not sell the TV program and get the public to tune in to watch the competition or event."

Adds Katarina Witt, "Skaters like Brian [Boitano] and I, we're the last generation that competed and skated for the sake of skating and never for the hope for a great paycheck. I feel like I'm a part of *The Last of the Mohicans*.

"For me, skating was a sport to collect medals. And I wanted more and more of them. It was never about how famous you can get or the endorsements you can have."

When it's all said and done, though, most legends realize and accept amateurs making money as just part of the reality of modern sports. After all, it isn't just figure skating. Before the 1976 Olympics, decathlete Bruce Jenner worked in an insurance company. Today's track and field stars have multi-million dollar endorsement deals.

"Honestly, it has changed for the better, and I think it's great that these kids have these opportunities," says Orser. "You know, I've had opportunities that the people before me didn't have. And it's just going to keep going on and evolving like that."

Along with the pay scale, the technical level has been taken up several notches in the last decade—most noticeably in the men's event, where, if you don't have a quad, you scarcely stand a chance.

That's a tall order in and of itself, but that's only half of today's demand. The judges are looking for a complete package: an athlete and an artist.

Is it fair to expect skaters to keep up with the technical advances and flourish creatively too?

"It's ridiculous," declares Boitano. "It's a jumping contest, and

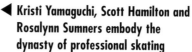
Kristi Yamaguchi, Scott Hamilton and Rosalynn Sumners embody the dynasty of professional skating

At the Masters of Figure Skating, ▶ their final competition as skater and coach: Michelle Kwan and Frank Carroll

◀ Mark Lund with CNN anchor Carol Lin in Salt Lake City during the 2002 Olympic Winter Games

ra Moskvina gets a lift from *Champions on* ▶ *Ice* executive producer Tom Collins (l) and al manager David Sutton backstage in 2001

◀ Michelle Kwan, Christine Brennan, Mark Lund and Lynn Plage at *A Skating Tribute: The Legacy of the 1961 U.S. World Team*, in New York's Madison Square Garden on October 5, 2001

Skating's most private duo: ▶
Ilia Kulik and Ekaterina Gordeeva

◀ Coaches and one father watch the warm-up for the women's free skate at 2002 U.S. Nationals

◀ ISU President Ottavio Cinquanta with World and Olympic judge Alla Shekhovtseva and her husband, Valentin Piseev, president of the Figure Skating Federation of Russia

Former New York mayor Rudolph Giuliani (c) ▶ addresses a crowd that includes JoJo Starbuck and Prince Andrew for the 2001 opening of the rink at Rockefeller Plaza

◀ Rudy Galindo brings down the house again with his often-used Village People medley

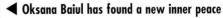
◀ Oksana Baiul has found a new inner peace

Cast members from *Toy Story* mix sports in ▶
Hawaii: (l-r) Jim Williams, Michelle Frenchville,
Larissa Zamotina and Craig Heath

◀ Skate Canada president Mar
Chidlow, David Pelletier and
Salé & Pelletier's then-mana
Craig Fenech at 2001 World

The IMG table at the 2001 Worlds banquet: (seated, l-r) Clair Brand, Natasha Pearson, Chris Abrey, Sindi Schorr (from sponsor Cafe de Colombia) and Liza Costanza; (standing, l-r) Dmitri Goryachkin,, Yuki Saegusa, Jay Ogden, Hiromi Motohashi and Andras Sallay

Scene from the underwhelmingly received 2002 ▶
Stars on Ice tour: Yamaguchi, Witt and Lipinski

◀ Star of the present: Alexei Yagudin

◄ The girl who has it all: Sarah Hughes adeptly juggles skating, school and celebrity

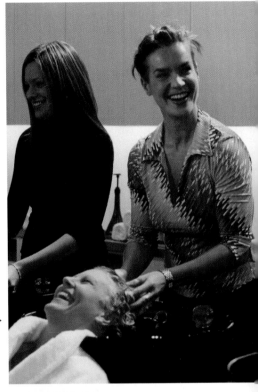

A humorous feature segment for ►
Katarina Witt's *Divas on Ice*

◄ John LeFevre, Claire Ferguson and Jerry Lace at a 2001 Worlds reception

◄ Jamie Salé & David Pelletier in their first press conference following the Olympic Pair free skate

Kristi Yamaguchi at an event produced ► by her Always Dream Foundation

◄ Tara Lipinski cultivates her hip and stylish image

◀ Nancy Kerrigan holds her decisive spot in skating royalty

One of skating's most unbreakable teams: ▶
Linda Leaver and Brian Boitano

◀ Steve Disson in motion

Months before its demise, SFX showed its ▶
strength at a charity golf tournament

It's better live™

that's what amateur skating is about. Skating should just admit it, instead of saying they are trying to make it more creative.

"No one can truly do what is being asked and on a consistent level. They don't have time to establish a character in a program, they don't have time to show edge quality. They are busy going back and forth and jumping, and that's what it's about. That's what it should be about. But don't pretend that it's something else."

Two-time U.S. Champion Michael Weiss, who is currently on the eligible scene, begs to differ. "It's difficult, but two people, [Alexei] Yagudin and [Evgeni] Plushenko, have been able to—time and again—master both of them," Weiss says. "So I don't think it's an unrealistic expectation for the judges to have on us. It is certainly attainable.

"Plus, it teaches the younger skaters that only working on quads won't get them a World title. A good example is the Chinese skaters. They will go out there and consistently perform two quads in a program and have yet to break into the medals at the World Championships. They need to work on the artistry and other areas, like spinning stronger and faster. Their programs need to be better. The judges have obviously said that they want the well-rounded skater. They want the skater that can do the quads and look good doing it."

Timothy Goebel, the 2002 Olympic Men's bronze medalist, says being able to pace oneself is the key factor in whether you have success or you crash and burn in the high-risk men's event.

"You have to find a balance between putting in the technical difficulty and still having enough left to skate a good, complete program. Besides all the jumps, we need to have interesting footwork and good spins. Pacing a program and having a little rest somewhere in there are so important, because it takes so much energy to do technical elements, that if you don't watch it, you're really too tired at the end to do anything well," Goebel explains.

"To have enough energy to do the choreography really well, with all the technical requirements, is something that I think is always going to be hard for a judge to find and an athlete to achieve."

Kulik also knows firsthand that the tricky balancing act is a lot to handle—and handle well. "The jump difficulty definitely cuts down on the artistry, because you cannot relax that much, which makes you more introverted. You're thinking more and concentrating more on the ice; you cannot really open up.

"This behavior starts being a habit, even after you've done the quad and difficult jump combination. It carries over to when you do the stuff that's a little bit easier. The habit is already there to be a little more inside yourself."

Yagudin, who is considered to be a superb artist, has admitted that at certain competitions, he has become so focused on conserving his energy in order to land all the jumps cleanly, he's omitted some of the footwork and other choreography.

This inclination is exactly what concerns Witt, who believes the personalities of the skaters now are being lost amid the requirements.

"Sure, it's incredible what they now do technically, but people remember emotions and what your vision is," she says. "Honestly, somebody who watches seven or eight triple jumps, plus the quads, may remember the amazing athletics, but they don't remember how they felt about it, because it may not have touched them.

"When the sport is taken too much out of the people's imagination, when you cannot relate to it anymore, it becomes almost frustrating, and it doesn't make it interesting anymore. And I think figure skating is a sport where you want to make people imagine and dream."

Another by-product of the increased emphasis on the jumps is that other technical elements are falling by the wayside, assesses Gardner.

"What has happened is there's no quality spinning, there's no quality edge work, which means there's no quality skating."

Adds Orser, "People come up to me all the time and comment how skating is all about the jumps and there's not as much interesting skating maneuvers as there used to be."

Denise Biellmann, the 1981 World Women's Champion, worries about a most practical dilemma: what the technical demands do to the skaters physically.

"They are being asked to do so many jumps, so they must focus so much on that aspect of their skating. The result is they have more injuries, and some skaters burn out much quicker than before," she states. "It's really a shame."

At the same time, Kulik feels that above all else, skating has to progress.

"Figure skating has to go forward difficulty-wise—that is the essence of sport," he says. "And in a couple of years, quads will be so easy and common, skaters will start to relax a little more, and their personalities will shine through.

"Then the cycle will repeat itself, and a couple more quads will probably be expected. It's the natural way of singles skating."

Meanwhile, ice dancers are facing their own challenges, as, in an attempt to quantify the discipline and make it easier to judge, the ISU has placed increased requirements and restrictions on the content of their programs.

"Personally, I was not upset by new regulations or new rules, just because they push you all the more to get far in your imagination to come up with new ideas and new moves. Sometimes, you come up with moves that you wouldn't have thought of if you were completely free," reasons Gwendal Peizerat, the 2002 Olympic Ice Dance Champion.

"You have to be willing to play with the rules and not to twist them, but get to the limits of the rules and to find new ideas."

What he would like to see in ice dance is the freedom to explore more modern dances. "If they keep the [13] limitations we have in the free dance, but at the same time we could do whatever we want in terms of style, that would lead to new, interesting programs," he says.

2001 World Ice Dance Champion Barbara Fusar-Poli wonders if the new limitations and requests are even being taking into consideration.

"Last season, the judges asked all the dance couples to please do a dance, not a drama. So we followed this request, as did the Canadians (Bourne and Kraatz). But the teams who didn't do a dance and stuck with dramatics, like the French (Anissina and Peizerat) and Russians (Lobacheva and Averbukh), were consistently judged better."

Ice dance legend Christopher Dean has mixed feelings about what he now sees in his sport.

"There are all these elements that have to be complied with, and they become a challenge to work around: the circular step sequence, the straight-line sequence and so many lifts. That does give you some basis to judge against, but creativity is in how each person tries to do something," Dean states.

"I do wonder, though, with everybody doing the same thing ... am I for it or against it? I'm neither. I understand why it's there, but sometimes it seems that people just stick a step sequence in, as opposed to really painting a picture.

"If someone is painting a picture, you wouldn't tell them each time, I want a table, a chair and a dog in it. No matter how you do it, that's what I want to see in the picture each time. You're just seeing the same picture, but moved around—as opposed to a different picture.

"What the ISU is trying to do is narrow it down to make it easier to judge, which you can understand," he continues. "One person likes Picasso, another person likes Matisse. They're trying to quantify skating in general, so the audience can look at it and understand it, and recognize, that's the lift, that's the step sequence, etc. It's an education of sorts. I personally liked it with more freedom and with the vastness of everyone trying to do something different."

Besides the new requirements, ice dancers this past season were faced with a peculiar order, one that left them scratching their heads.

"At the European Championships, we received this directive to skate your entire programs in practice. This was the very first time this was done. Usually what we do is to do part of our programs on different days. The goal is for us to be able to perform everything on the ice before the competition so the judges who haven't seen it before can have a general vision of the whole thing," says Peizerat.

"What happened is that some judges complained and said some of the skaters would always only do the same parts of the program and didn't show the rest," he adds. "So by the time of the competition, the judges wouldn't have seen all of the required elements of each program. That's why they came up with the idea of having a practice where the skaters would have to perform all of the elements of their program, but not the entire program. The trouble is, if you count all the required elements, and if your program is balanced, the elements are every 15 seconds.

"If you were to do the elements one at a time, you would just skate, then stop, skate, then stop. That would kill the flow of the program. So you have the choice to perform the whole thing or be very clever and find a way to show all of the elements.

"At the draw at Europeans, Povilas Vanagas (2000 European and World bronze medalist from Lithuania) asked, 'What if I don't perform at one of the two practices, what will happen to me?' The referee told him, 'You better do both of them, because I asked you to.' At Europeans, we all did this, though we were pretty upset about it. But also, we joked a lot about it, that it was like a pre-competition.

"When we told the free skaters about this, they said, 'You ice dancers are so quiet and respectful of all the rules. We free skaters would never do it. They would never ask us to do it, because nobody would ever do it. No one.' This is true. We were the good kids."

This directive didn't quite work as well at the Olympics. "With everyone arriving at different times to Salt Lake, it was hard for the referees to get the skaters to do this. What was the most disappointing was that whether they asked for the skaters to do this, some of the judges wouldn't even show up. We had only three to four coming to a practice that was done especially for them. In the dressing room, that was the big joke," notes Peizerat.

What's not funny at all to Scott Hamilton is the way eligible skaters today are wearing out the welcome mat by not moving on.

Instead of progressing through eligible skating into the professional realm, skaters are grabbing the available opportunities to maintain their amateur status and, in effect, impeding the traditional succession of champions. In some ways, it's just survival. With fewer and fewer professional opportunities, staying eligible is the only way to protect your livelihood.

"When you're 18, and you see the guy who's the champion is 30, you think, *Am I going to have to wait until I'm 30?* When you look at how long a lot of these skaters stay in now, because they can make a lot of money, it's not natural. In a way, it's hurting the sport, because the next skater, the new excitement, the next champion, isn't coming in and inheriting the throne," Hamilton declares.

"They're having to wait longer without that logical transition that used to take place. I think it hurts a lot of the younger skaters coming up. They think, *If I don't make it now, I'll never make it,* because once a skater is there, he or she is going to stay there for eight, nine or even 10 years.

"Admittedly, Michelle Kwan has done an amazing job of being the people's champion, but you wonder when that's going to start to run out. Do they want to see Sarah Hughes next? Do they want to see Sasha Cohen? Is it time for Michelle to think about allowing the next champion to develop and for her to go on to develop the next aspect of her career?

"Those aren't my decisions to make, but there used to be this logical transition from you were that (amateur) and now you're this (professional). And you can build something that is absolutely yours and unique and lasting that goes beyond your competitive years," Hamilton explains.

"Bottom line, what's happening isn't at all good for the sport. You really do need a logical transition of champions. And these skaters have to be made to understand that."

Good luck, says 1983 World Women's Champion Rosalynn Sumners. She contends the younger generation of skaters would likely turn a deaf ear.

"In this day and age, if I gave young skaters advice, they wouldn't listen," asserts Sumners. "I don't think they would listen to

Scott Hamilton's advice either. It is a different generation, and on the whole, I don't think they quite have the respect, because they feel they are such big deals."

She concedes, however, that this change in skaters' attitudes has a lot to do with the way they are treated by the public. "The whole media is so different now than when we were coming up, because they turn them into stars faster, which affects the mentality," Sumners says.

Besides the increased media interest and expectations, eligible skaters today face more competitions, thanks to the Grand Prix series.

"We worked hard, but what these skaters are doing right now in one year is considerably more than I ever did in one season," assesses Sumners. "They have to get tired."

Adds Hamilton, "There is also pressure on these skaters now to compete more with their biggest competitors than ever before, which can take its toll."

Yagudin knows this all too well. He rode a roller coaster of feelings en route to his Olympic gold medal in Salt Lake City.

"I might be so emotional one time and then just really calm, because I was realizing that this is the Olympic season. I knew that I had to win a lot before going to the Olympics to be sure that it would be easier. So the whole year was full of emotion, from the Goodwill Games to the Europeans to the Olympic finals. There was so much pressure, I was like, 'Don't talk to me,' or 'OK, like, let's talk,'" shares Yagudin.

All of the changes in eligible skating point to one thing, says Sumners.

"I don't think they will carry their careers as long and far into the pro ranks, because they are already making major money," she contends. "What is the motivation? For us, we were building something, and the money was getting better. That was the motivation. As opposed to, what's the new generation's motivation to go on? The sport is established and the money is already here."

To today's skaters who may think they're hot stuff, history may not be so kind.

"Fans of skating and the general public that follow the sport will always know who Scott Hamilton, Katarina Witt, Brian Boitano and Kristi Yamaguchi are. Three years from now they could very easily say 'Sasha who?'" says Sumners.

Jerry Solomon, Nancy Kerrigan's husband and agent, agrees 100 percent.

"On January 6th of every year, since 1994, there are specials and notes in the paper; a big deal is made of that day [when Nancy was attacked at U.S. Nationals]. CNN even runs something every year. I guarantee you that 10 years from now, no one will be saying on February whatever, today's the 10th anniversary of the Salé and Pelletier double gold medal. Not going to happen," he asserts.

The current star power simply doesn't shine as bright, says Boitano.

"There is a quality that people talk about, an electric attitude that someone has that makes you compelled to watch them. Usually, when you look at a star skater, you feel that way. There's just something about Katarina's skating or someone else's skating you can't put your finger on, but you just like it, or the audience just likes it. That's what makes someone a star. And that's what's truly missing right now," he assesses.

"I think that if Michelle had won the Olympics, she would have been like a Katarina or a Kristi. It's a combination of people really liking you, having the achievement, liking your personality, liking your skating and having that electric energy."

Kristi Yamaguchi notes, "Katarina can walk into a room and

everyone's head turns. It's a certain charisma that she has. Brian [Boitano] has that same presence. You don't see that every day."

Unfortunately, says Solomon, what we do see frequently now is that the women's champions are getting younger and younger.

"They are 15 and 16 years old, which we know historically from gymnastics and other sports of that kind, that age [for] a champion does not bring with it a real following," offers Solomon. "Adult spectators do not really enjoy watching children."

So as the legends pass the torch—albeit perhaps a little hesitantly—to the new kids on the block, what's their parting message?

Recommends Sumners, "Enjoy it. Appreciate where it came from. But please don't blow it."

1994

"The energy was very tabloid-esque. It was *Access Hollywood* and Connie Chung at the rail trying to get Tonya or Nancy to talk. It was a little disconcerting. To the press, their soap opera was the Winter Games."

– Brian Boitano, 1994 Men's competitor, 1988 Olympic Men's gold medalist

1994

A media frenzy swept through the 1994 Lillehammer Olympics like a Category Five hurricane.

Caught in the eye of that storm was Nancy Kerrigan, the victim of skating history's most famous whack on the knee. In the end, she came through with flying colors and by the narrowest of margins lost the gold medal to Ukrainian orphan Oksana Baiul, who became the skating world's new darling. Tonya Harding's cries of innocence in Kerrigan's attack fell on deaf ears—and she fell apart in the competition.

More than 78 million people tuned in to watch that women's final, which provided a bump for the sport like nothing before or since. Kerrigan, then 24, and Baiul, just 16, became adored by the masses and put on a pedestal that neither one wanted or was prepared to handle.

For Kerrigan, the strain showed immediately.

Her impatience waiting for the medal ceremony was on display during the CBS broadcast. A few days later, exasperation set in during a Disney World parade. The sound blurb played ad nauseam by the media was Kerrigan announcing, "This is the corniest thing I've done in my life," while riding on a float with Mickey Mouse. The public wasn't amused at the crack seemingly directed at the nation's most cherished animated icon. Later on she said the remark actually was about wearing her Olympic silver medal. But by then no one was listening.

Not surprisingly, Nancy doesn't look back with any fondness on her time under the media microscope. "For me it was intimidating. Some people thrive on it and love it. I didn't," she declares.

"Right from the time the competition finished, people were ready to be critical of me. I found it very scary. It was like I became that kid again who was really shy, because I had to be quiet," reveals Nancy. "I thought, if I say anything, someone's going to take it the wrong way or splice my 10-minute conversation into one sentence and change it around and now it's negative."

It wasn't paranoia talking. It was reality. An incident that still sticks in Kerrigan's mind occurred right after she flew from Lillehammer to do four hours of satellite interviews, which began at 6:00 a.m.

"I was exhausted. Weeks and weeks of media, media, media; people following me everywhere I go. Finally, I was just tired and my body had let go. I sat in a chair between interviews and yawned," she recalls. "A simple, natural act, especially early in the morning. The next thing I know, it's on one of those shows, implying I'm unappreciative because I did it."

Those who know Nancy feel she was simply given a bad rap by the press.

"Honestly, Nancy deserved more than she got at those Olympics. She just wanted to do her job after this terrible incident, which she just couldn't talk or hear about anymore. She just wanted to move on," explains friend Katarina Witt. "It was a very, very difficult situation. I feel sorry that she was so misinterpreted by so many people. Probably, she was only trying to protect herself by how she behaved."

Brian Boitano concurs. "Nancy has always been honest and says it like it is. A lot of times people misunderstood that. Once you meet her, you understand. She just speaks straight off the cuff. That's her way."

It was a true learning experience for Kerrigan. "I'd just skated all my life. I'm not very complicated. I'm never out to get anyone. People have been helpful to me. I just skate and I try to be a good person," she says.

"I don't understand the need to look for something bad when someone's just a nice person going about their business. I didn't have time to get into trouble when I was a kid between skating, school and work. I'm boring, but I never intended to be exciting, except on the ice. So the press made things up."

It was déjà vu for Nancy as she sat at home watching the controversial pair decision at the 2002 Winter Games and the media barrage that followed. "I had so many phone calls. Everybody wanted to talk to me and I wasn't involved at all," she marvels. "Since as far back as *The Boston Globe* goes in 1908, there's been controversy in figure skating. The difference this year was the Canadian federation really stuck behind their team. In the past everyone just accepted it."

That's exactly what she had done in Lillehammer. "I lost by one tenth of a point even though I had much more content and technical difficulty. It was just OK. No one said, 'Wait a minute! Let's go over this, this isn't right.' If they had, maybe things might have changed," she offers.

Instead, what Nancy chose to focus on was how well she persevered through the media onslaught to deliver the two finest performances of her career. Her husband and manager Jerry Solomon, whom she wed in September 1995, calls it the zone. "He says he's seen very few people able to get in such a place," she says. "It was like I was in a tunnel. For six weeks I concentrated on my focus, getting better, healing and skating how I'd been trained to do."

Nancy, however, concedes that without all the attention perhaps she wouldn't have found her zone. "You can't just get yourself there. I think you have to have something happen to force it inside of you."

On the other hand, her unique circumstances were trying. Nancy didn't feel part of a team like she had at the 1992 Olympics, where she won a bronze medal. "In '94, I didn't get to march in the opening ceremonies because of the knee. It was cold. The doctors didn't want me walking on it. Then I was asked not to do the closing ceremonies (due to death threats). It was very disappointing," she admits. "All of the attention was very suffocating, isolating and hard to deal with."

As for her feelings toward the woman, then a girl, who beat her for Olympic gold? "I've never had a problem with Oksana. People always thought I would because she won. I felt the judges made the decision. She did a nice job and she was very cute."

After the Lillehammer Olympics, skating skyrocketed to the second most popular sport in America. Pro competitions and special events popped up all over TV. "It was a feeding frenzy, and I was a part of it. I remember being thanked by Peter Carruthers (1984 Olympic Pair silver medalist–turned–TV commentator). He said, 'Thank you so much, because I have so much work now,'" she recalls.

Unquestionably, Nancy's continued presence was key to skating's popularity explosion. "There were times when people would say, 'You have to do the event, because if you don't do it, the sponsor doesn't want to do the event.' I felt tired and I didn't want to go, but the producers would say, 'We really want you there; we really need you because all these other people want to do the event.' So I'd agree to go."

Nancy says there was no time for her to separate herself from this craziness. "I was so busy. I think I worked for more than 23 companies at once, so I wasn't just doing the shows and the tours and the competitions at the time. In between, I was making appearances. I had come out with my children's book, and I was doing a book tour along with the *Champions on Ice* tour. I didn't even have a day off the entire tour because I was always doing something," she remembers.

Responsible for fielding the plentiful offers coming Nancy's way, Jerry Solomon found himself in familiar territory. He has represented such high profile athletes as world-number-one tennis players Pete Sampras and Ivan Lendl. "The issues were different, but the volume and type of activities were similar. The only thing out of the ordinary was the short period of time surrounding Nancy's attack in Detroit," he says.

"Also, I think that to a certain extent what was happening was more fast and furious for the people outside than it was for us. If you come from a background like Nancy's where you didn't have anything to begin with and you're not particularly concerned about having money, you don't feel the pressure to make a decision to go do something that's going to pay you X amount of dollars—or if you don't make a decision by a certain date you'll lose the money. We always had time to take a step back and laugh about it and enjoy it and talk about it," Jerry offers.

Her grounded upbringing also made Nancy keenly aware of the fortunate position she was in, so she chose to embrace the zaniness swirling around her and skating. "That big eruption of excitement doesn't last that long. It's still exciting, but it's just not the same level. I told Sarah Hughes she had to do the *Champions on Ice* tour because it won't be the same for her next year. Yes, the crowd will still love you, clap and think you're great, but it's not like, 'Wow!' when there is an eruption kind of feeling."

Nancy contends that defining her daily routine proved the hardest aspect of her transition to life as a pro skater. "Before, I got up every morning and did this much skating and worked out. All of a sudden I didn't have to, so why am I getting up that early," she says that she wondered.

She feels her connection with the audience has improved immeasurably as a professional. "You can't stare down at the ice and try to forget they're there and concentrate to do the program like you do at home, which is a real tendency as an eligible skater. You can't do that when you're performing. You have to do it big and full of life so that you're reaching the people way up at the top of the seats."

Unlike skaters who took pro competitions as seriously as ones in their eligible days, Nancy just wanted to have fun. "People like Kristi [Yamaguchi] trained for those competitions. I got ready for the performance. I like that aspect and didn't want to do the same kind of training I did for the Olympics. It was about performing in front of an audience and seeing my skating friends that I hadn't seen in a long time."

Nancy also had a differing opinion when it came to skaters' appearance fees. "I had suggested that we should only be paid prize money in pro competitions. No one agreed with me. People don't want to give up things that are comfortable," she charges.

"OK, maybe because I'm there I should still get something, but I certainly shouldn't be making more money than the girl that won! Then it's not really sport. By that point you don't need to go home with a trophy because you're going home with a check. Wouldn't you keep more of an edge and make for a more exciting competition if your money hinged on your placement? I think the public knew what was going on, and it hurt skating."

Nancy famously made similar remarks during a CBS competition telecast in the fall of 1995, upsetting Scott Hamilton and other skaters. In her trademark honest style, Nancy had disclosed skating's biggest secret at the time—it had become a big business.

It wasn't long into her pro career that Nancy and Jerry opted to create their own projects, ones aspiring to be different from the traditional skating productions. In 1995, they launched the annual *Halloween on Ice* show, a fitting venture since Oct. 31 is Nancy's birthday. Then two years ago, Kerrigan jumped at the chance to do a theatrical skating show based on the 1980s hit movie *Footloose*. She was contacted by Renaissance Entertainment, with which she now partners in the 900-seat Ice Castle Theatre in Myrtle Beach, S.C.

"I absolutely loved doing *Footloose on Ice*. I love that kind of performance and being on stage. Performing and being on the ice more than four minutes and playing a character throughout a show—I love that. And on top of that you're still doing all the athletics and skating," enthuses Nancy.

In addition to facing the creative challenges of performing onstage, she was integrally involved in all aspects of the production.

"Working with her, I've really seen her grow as a performer," notes Randy Gardner, who served as the choreographer-director for both *Halloween on Ice* and *Footloose on Ice*. "I'm very pleased to see that she stays involved from A to Z. I think it gives her a whole new avenue and keeps things interesting for her."

With skating's appeal decreasing to the pre-1994 norm, the current pro scene has become increasingly territorial. Many skaters and business people were staking claim to what little turf is left. Unlike most, Nancy finds herself in a great position. She has carved a unique niche by creating her own skating productions and developing other interests with business pursuits in mind, including painting and pottery. And most importantly, she's having a blast.

"You think about athletes, you think, stick to what you do. Or you think because you're an athlete or you're a singer or something, you can't do all of these other things. Well, you're so focused on one thing for so long, you don't realize that you can actually do other things, because you've never developed those talents or those interests. It's really fun now to be less busy in skating and to find out these new things that I like. For instance, I didn't know that I could paint," shares Nancy.

Jerry has also enjoyed his wife spreading her wings. "Nancy is a somewhat unique individual in that she has tremendous talent in several other areas. So my job here is to figure out a way to allow her to transition into those areas where she really does have talent. That's sort of fun for me.

"The real question for Nancy, like most athletes, is will she ever have the motivation to work as hard at the next thing, whether it's singing or pottery or acting, as she worked at skating? Only time will tell. And most athletes who've been working at something since they were 10 years old, working full-time, for a long period of time—by the time they're 35 they say, 'You know I just don't want to work that hard at anything.' And that's understandable too," he says.

What struck Jerry most about Nancy at the beginning of their business relationship was her refreshing attitude. "When I was first hired to represent her, she was like, 'What do I need an agent for? What does an agent do?' So for me it was an opportunity to do a lot more directing and molding than with another athlete who either was more involved or more headstrong about certain things or had different ideas.

"We have a lot of respect for each other's talents and the areas in which we have them," Jerry adds. "There's good communication, so we're able to make those things mesh. Not to say we always agree, but sometimes that's part of the fun of it, for me anyway. And we're doing the things that we like to do."

One of the things Kerrigan and Solomon unquestionably do as a team is raise their 6-year-old son, Matthew. For Nancy, being a mother is a dream come true and her number one priority.

"Matthew always comes first in my life," she says. "I had a great role model in my own mother, and I am very thankful and grateful for that." In May of 2001, The National Mother's Day Council selected Nancy as one of five national recipients of the Outstanding Mother of the Year award. "It was quite an honor, for an organization like this to recognize me for doing a good job in this area that is so important to me."

Nancy would like to have more children. "It's so hard when you have a career and you plan, 'OK, now it's time to have the baby.' Ideally, I would have been done having babies by now. I would have had four," she offers. In early 2002 she suffered a miscarriage, but doctors assure her she can try again to get pregnant.

Nancy's fame has allowed her to do something she always wanted: to give back. She established the Nancy Kerrigan Foundation in honor of her mother, Brenda Kerrigan, who is legally blind. The Foundation distributes funds to various charities that support the visually impaired. At the time of its inception Nancy said, "I'm really excited about honoring my mom in this way. She's always been very supportive of me and I'm thrilled to support others in her name."

In 2000, she started the Nancy Kerrigan Pro-Celebrity Golf Classic with proceeds benefiting her foundation. "I love to be able to help people," shares Nancy. "People used to say to me, 'What are you skating for? What do you get back?' When I was young, there weren't the opportunities there are now. The opportunities sort of came along when I did. So now I can say, 'See, it was all worth something. I can actually do something. I can help somebody.'"

"Her commitment to the tournament wasn't just her name," says Jane Blalock, a former professional golfer who owns the golf marketing company that produced Kerrigan's tournament. "She played. She was there early. She stayed late. She did interviews prior to the event. She was accessible."

Last year Nancy also lent her time to the sport surface nearest to her heart. She starred in "Ice Angels for Kelly," a benefit show at her hometown Stoneham, Mass., rink, with proceeds going to a local teenager in need of a lung transplant. "I feel doing something worthwhile and helping somebody is the greatest thing I've been able to do because of my skating," says Nancy.[1]

Recently, Nancy's good deeds have been recognized by two philanthropic organizations. On March 12, 2001, she was presented with the "People of Vision Award" at the Boston Billiards Club Benefit for Blindness. And this past spring, she, along with Indianapolis Colts quarterback Peyton Manning, was a recipient of the Henry P. Iba Citizen Athlete Award. Athletes are chosen for this award because of their commitment to being a positive role model and their contributions to charity.

"Nancy has really made a wonderful transition to being a mom and being a producer, plus the things she is doing now for charity. She is happier than I have seen her in a really long time," shares long-time friend Paul Wylie, who, like Nancy, was coached by Evy and Mary Scotvold. "I remember her as this person who really loved to skate, different when you got to know her from what the rest of the world saw. She was a fantastic training partner. I got several notes while I was skating, encouraging me through tough times, and I was there when she was getting yelled at by Evy for whatever reason. We bonded in a way that you do when there is only one other person who knows how you're feeling about something."

Growing up, Nancy never imagined the people she could meet, places she could go and lives she could touch through skating. "How would I ever think that I would be one of the two or three people that went to the Olympics? I couldn't feel like that coming from my background, because there easily might be somebody better than me," she explains. "And I'm still skating at my age. I never expected anything like what I've gotten from figure skating."

In the final analysis, Nancy isn't too concerned with her place in the record books, but rather how she approached her sport. "I want to be remembered as a hard worker and someone that tried hard and enjoyed it and was entertaining."

Her candor won't be forgotten either.

"What I love about Nancy is what you see is what you get. If she's in a bad mood, she shows it to you. I like that. I don't want any bullshit. I don't want somebody who is kind to my face, and then behind my back they are going to be dishonest," states

Katarina Witt. "In the last couple of years she is so much more comfortable, and that's what shows. I always see her smile and laugh or be in a good mood. She has a great family with Matthew and Jerry. She's on a really good path."

Oksana Baiul, too, has found peace and harmony in her life today, but it was a long, rocky road.

"It's publicly known she had very little guidance. She grew up with virtually nothing financially, and she was able to make a lot of money after winning the gold medal. She simply got too much too soon. She was 16 years old and didn't know how to handle it and had a lot of vultures around her. A lot of people were trying to get a part of her money, but there was very little stability around her," asserts Dr. Francis Lodato, Baiul's psychologist for the past five years.

At age 17, Oksana purchased a spacious home in Connecticut just for her. "I did it because all my friends who were around me at that point of my life were older. They were 25 and they had kids and family. I thought that if they are buying houses that is what I am supposed to do," she explains.

It was a move she would regret. "It turned out to be a big f---ing party house! Everybody was coming over, having free meals, drinks—and of course, I would buy that stuff. I would wake up, and I was supposed to go to the ice rink, and I would see some-body in the kitchen preparing breakfast and I would say, 'Oh, I thought you left last night, but you are still here,'" describes Oksana. "For me, in a way, it was like I was trying to buy myself happiness. That is what I thought at that time in my life.

"It wasn't a good idea for me to make such a purchase, but I could afford it—and nobody stopped me. It would have been wonderful if I had a family to live in that home, but I didn't have anybody." She eventually sold the house and ultimately bought herself a one-bed-room condominium in New Jersey.

What kept Oksana going during her early days of fame and fortune was the feeling she got from performing, particularly on Tom Collins' *Champions on Ice* tour. "To step out on the ice night after night in the show came a sense of love. Then, that was what I lived for," she shares.

"Later on, when I was 22 or 23, I realized that I was madly searching for love from the audience because I missed my mother's. Skating filled the void."

Oksana feels substituting skating for her lack of family was a major factor in her ice triumphs. "Everybody has good days and bad days, but the other kids had parents to turn to if they had a bad performance. The bad performance didn't stay with them. For me, the performances were all I had, so I guess that's why I became so good at it. I was a perfectionist."

Increasingly, after the Olympics, Oksana began to struggle with the closest thing to family she had, her surrogate mother figure and coach, Galina Zmievskaya. The media romanticized the complicated relationship between the two, which proved to be a real bone of contention for Oksana.

"Until the short program at the Olympics, the media had no idea who I was. In the two days before the long program they wanted to learn and create something for the public. They were like, 'She is Ukrainian. She is an orphan. So who is her guardian?' They focused on Galina," she explains.

It made for a good tale. Also competing in Lillehammer was Galina's other star pupil, her son-in-law Viktor Petrenko, the 1992 Olympic Men's Champion, who paid for many of Oksana's personal expenses. It was Viktor and Galina, says Oksana, who were responsible for providing CBS with information for the movie about her life in which quite the family picture was painted.

"I was 16 at the time and had no idea what was going on. I wasn't telling the story," responds Baiul. "To this day I still do not know whether Galina was legally my guardian or not."

What she does know and regrets is that her other coach, Valentin Nikolaev, was ignored by the media—and Galina. "When Galina decided we should come to America, to tell you the truth I was working on only my artistic impression with her. The real coach was Valentin. That's the real story, and that when we came to this country, Galina forgot about this coach and left him behind," states Oksana.

Oksana is not ungrateful to Galina. "She did some wonderful things for me when I was young. Without her, I think I would never, ever have come to this country that I love. Now, it's my home." (Baiul is currently taking steps to become a U.S. citizen.)

But along the way something happened. "I felt that she was just taking too much money for whatever she was doing for me. She would take 30% of my money, and that, I think, was too much. A little bit too much from everything that I would make in skating," declares Oksana.

"I could definitely see that the meal ticket part of their relationship was an important one. Oksana is not wrong to feel that way," confirms Michael Carlisle, Oksana's agent from 1994–98.

"When we did the jewelry line, Galina wasn't getting any money on the endorsements. Oksana got 100 percent of it. They were not large endorsements, but we had a clothing line for a little while, too," he states. "I tried to develop a side that was outside of Galina, that was to Americanize Oksana, if you will, and introduce her to other aspects of entertainment. Galina always disliked that. She felt like it was a waste if it didn't involve skating."

Oksana feels Galina pushed her hard, too hard, to do what Galina wanted—even if it meant skating while hurt. While at a summer ice show in Sun Valley, Idaho, in 1994, Oksana injured her knee and she underwent arthroscopic surgery. Looming large that fall were many skating opportunities for Oksana, and by association, Galina. "My agency told me that Galina was coming to their office and saying stuff like, 'You have to make her come to work.' She was screaming at me and the agency was saying, 'OK, if she is not capable of doing this, she is not supposed to.'"

"All of the decisions as to what she would skate and where she would skate were made by Galina, not with Galina. So the representation was of Oksana as directed or managed by Galina," says Carlisle.

This arrangement didn't set well at all with Oksana, who felt she needed to grow as a skater, and at one point she confronted Galina about wanting to try new things. "I told her, 'I need to grow as an artist and need to entertain people. This is not about winning the gold anymore. Now it is an entertainment business.' She wouldn't listen. I don't blame her though, because she doesn't know anything better than that."

By November of 1996, Oksana was effectively estranged from Galina. That year she spent Thanksgiving with Carlisle. "It was Oksana and my family, and she kind of hadn't been in a family environment like that for a very long time. And that's what she wanted. I felt very sad for her," he shares.

"Galina was a very important part of her life, and very good for her in her life because she was a mother substitute. She gave her a little bit of stability. But there was kind of a delayed adolescence with Oksana, and she rebelled against anybody telling her what to do and that kind of led to the breakdown between her and Galina," describes Dr. Lodato. "It was just a typical dependence/independence conflict between an adolescent and a surrogate parent. She was living with Galina, and Galina had some rules. I never saw it as being any more serious than that, but maybe Oskana never understood it completely."

"I think Galina tried hard to take a child who was pretty wild and pretty screwed up and take her into her family and bring her into some kind of a structure," assesses Carlisle. "There was this sense that what Oksana had, she was wasting."

"I did everything in my power to help this girl," Galina says. "I took her into my family. She had all my parental love, just like my own daughters. She had the same food, same bed sheets, same everything.

"I was her coach," she adds. "Everyone knows that."

Galina says there was no formal guardianship. She declines to comment on what percentage of Oksana's skating earnings she received. She does not dispute that she insisted Oksana continue to skate when she was injured.

"Many skaters get injured, and they continue to skate," she says. "I wouldn't do it, if I thought it could hurt her.

"I will say this, when she was with me, she was a skater. What she became skating-wise after we split, everyone knows."

No one realized just to what degree there were problems until everything came tumbling down.

In the early morning hours of Jan. 14, 1997, the 19-year-old crashed her Mercedes into a tree near her Connecticut home. Her blood alcohol level was .168, well above the state's legal limit of .02 for drivers under the age of 21.

Though lucky to escape with only minor injuries, Oksana faced a drunk driving arrest. She pled no contest to a reduced charge in exchange for undergoing alcohol education and volunteering for community service.

Like many young people, Oksana's drinking problem came about in part due to the crowd she ran with—one that drank a lot.

The crowd included some of the skaters on the Tom Collins' tour. "I just did what everybody was doing," explains Oksana.

"There was no one there to comment that she was out of control until it got to the point where it could not be denied any more. There was a lot of enabling done and people overlooked a lot of her behavior," says Dr. Lodato.

Interestingly, the only person on the tour Oksana recalls making any effort to detour her from alcohol was Nancy Kerrigan. One day Oksana grabbed a beer. "Nancy said, 'It's not good for you. Really, it's bad for you.' But, I was like 'No, it's OK for me,'" she recalls.

"She was a nice kid. You worried because she was so young," offers Nancy. "You didn't want anyone to take advantage of her. She would go off by herself and I would think 'Where are you going all alone?'"

As for Petrenko, Baiul states simply, "He's a decent guy"— though she admits he never talked with her about her drinking problem. "We never had a conversation that I should stop drinking or that drinking is bad for you."

Oksana also truly believes that, for her, drinking was just in her blood. "There is such an ability to drink in Russian culture. Besides, nobody really talked to me about drinking." She says that though she drowned herself in liquor, it was never a high for her. "It never felt good, never at any time in my life. I would just feel drunk and my head would spin. Plus, we were always working and traveling from city to city on the tour, so it never felt good."

As her drinking troubles came to a head, her stint with the *Champions on Ice* tour wound down. "I think Tommy really knew what was going on with me, but don't forget that he's not my father. He was the producer of the show. If I were the producer of the show, I would not be a very happy person to see somebody who is that talented and that young basically killing herself. In the end, business is business," reasons a realistic Oksana.

"Near the end of her being on the tour she would have these incredible mood swings. Happy to see you one minute, then don't dare to speak to her the next. It made things very uncomfortable because you didn't know how you could act around her and that made it hard on everybody," remembers Nancy. "When she got frustrated with herself, then she'd come in closer to you on the ice like she was going to hit you or something, so you didn't want to necessarily practice. But I think a lot of that action came from within herself and was not really about anyone else.

"She was troubled in a lot of ways, and on top of it all, she was a teenager and she was growing up. That's a hard thing to do with everybody watching."

Oksana characterizes her current relationship with Tom Collins as "wonderful." As for Nancy, she says, "She's a wonderful human being. She's definitely someone I could share a laugh with today."

Unbeknownst to Oksana at the time, her alcohol addiction also cost her a major endorsement contract, says Carlisle, who was then with the William Morris Agency. "Literally, we were talking numbers to finalize a six-figure phone card deal with one of the major companies and boom, it was gone after the accident. Oksana didn't know about it yet." The agency was left in a very awkward position. "Imagine negotiating for somebody and finding out they've become the most talked-about bad girl," cracks Carlisle.

Lost endorsements.

Dismissal from the *Champions on Ice* tour.

Rejection from the skating world.

Nothing seemed to deter Baiul from the bottle or wake her up to the fact that she was on a destructive, possibly deadly, path. "For a while I was still doing the same thing—drinking and driving—but I just never got caught again," she admits. It was the end of 1997 before she sought help. She began a relationship that continues to this day with Dr. Lodato, who encouraged her to get treatment for her alcohol addiction. Baiul entered Silver Hills, a private hospital in Connecticut, on April 30, 1998.

"Dr. Lodato is the one I owe a lot of thanks to. He's the one who took me by the hand and led me to rehab," Oksana explains. It proved quite an emotional day when she arrived at the hospital for admittance. "All of a sudden I got really quiet and Frank (Dr. Lodato) said, 'What's wrong with you?' I said, 'Do you think by going to this place I will die?'"

The doctor painted a realistic picture of Oksana's choices. "Frank told me, 'No, you won't die there if you will be very open, work hard and will try to change a lot of things about yourself. But if you don't go there, then you will die,'" recalls Oksana.

Her time at Silver Hills went beyond the customary 30 days. "Oksana opted to stay because she felt like she wasn't strong enough, and it was a very good decision on her part. She was there three months," says Dr. Lodato. "Oksana went through a 12-step program and some group counseling programs. She learned a lot about relationships and a lot of things about herself then."

Dr. Lodato reports that while Oksana is not actively involved in a 12-step program today, she has incorporated and internalized all the things she needed to do. "The fact is, she will always be a recovering alcoholic, but hopefully she gets stronger as she goes along the way," he says. "She has become very critical of people who are abusing alcohol and makes it known to people that she cares about that and maybe they should look at this."

In the end, Oksana became her own anchor and barometer of life. "People overlook that she is a very intelligent gal. She had very little formal education, but she is very insightful," assesses

Dr. Lodato. "I remember when she was in Silver Hills and she used to attack the reading assignments as if she were getting ready to do a thesis or an oral exam. She was well prepared every day. She read and read as much as she could. She participated very well."

The reaction by the skating community to the "new" Oksana, post rehab, was a positive one. "They were so cool. Honestly, I think they were happy because I was such a nightmare before," shares Oksana. "Before, I would run around in my pajamas all over the hotel and just act crazy.... I mean really disgusting. Afterwards, they were able to deal with me, and I could sit in one place and listen to what they had to say. I went back to being a normal human being."

She returned to *Champions on Ice* for two seasons before deciding to forgo touring for a home life.

Of all the offers that came her way after her recovery, one takes the cake for Oksana. Venerable skating agent Michael Rosenberg proposed that she pose for *Playboy* magazine.

"He offered me this right after I came out of rehab, I would do a full layout and cover for a million dollars," she declares. "I turned it down. It was inappropriate for me, especially after what I had just been through. Besides, I want to be remembered as a figure skater, not as a whore!"

When she was ready for more appropriate pursuits like resuming skating, Oksana turned to coach Valentin Nikolaev, the one who had sat to her left as she waited for her marks in Lillehammer. "From the time I came to America at 16 and up to 20, 21, I really didn't have a coach who would tell me how to jump, how to move or how to spin on the ice. Everybody thought Galina was doing that, but she wasn't. And I needed that," she says.

Nikolaev also helped Oksana deal with a major growth spurt, and made adjustments to her skating accordingly. When she won the Olympic gold medal she was a waiflike 4'11" and barely weighed 100 lbs. In the few years thereafter, she had grown five inches. "It was very, very tough, but I got through it. By the time I turned 20, I had stopped growing and gaining weight," she says. Oksana then went through a period where her weight fluctuated. Today, she maintains an ideal weight of 120 lbs.

In recent years, Baiul has distanced herself somewhat from skating and thrown herself into her personal life and taking care of herself. It was just what the doctor ordered. "I had been whining to Dr. Lodato that I was not happy. I was working so much, and basically I had been doing this since I was 16 years old, so I had thought maybe I should take a break and think about some other things. I just got burned out."

Shortly after she stopped touring, she met her fiancé, Eugene "Gene" Sunik, a Russian-born businessman who has lived in the U.S. for 25 of his 30 years.

Simply put, time away from life on the road has not exactly made her pine for its return. "Honestly, I like my stable life, and we just got a little puppy, a little Chihuahua. I am enjoying staying at one place and sleeping in my own bed, living a life and making food for Eugene," shares Oksana. "I enjoy doing that normal stuff and having normal hours. I think it's wonderful."

She does admit, though, that her desire to skate for an audience still burns. "Honest to God, I do miss performing! I think at some point I definitely will go back to it. Now, I am just taking time for myself."

Oksana hints that the return to the ice may be just around the corner. "I am working right now on something big and different than what I did before. I'm a skater, an entertainer. I need to do it." In early 2002, she signed on with a new agent, Peter Carlisle of Octagon, who she was parting with at year's end.

Meanwhile, she has kept her foot in the sport through her new line of skating apparel, the Oksana Baiul Collection, which debuted in the spring on her Web site and in August with retailers. "This year we decided to stick with figure skating, because I wanted to establish the brand and get a feel for the buyers. Next year we will go full force, including jogging suits, swimwear and accessories," explains Oksana.

Not only has Gene helped Oksana explore her aspirations beyond the ice, but he also gave her what she was most in need of and wanted desperately.

"By me being with Gene, I met family. He has a lot of relatives. I was always searching, wishing to find a family, and now I have," beams Oksana.

"When I was 7 years old, my grandfather passed away. When I was 9 years old, my grandmother passed away. When I was 13, my mom passed away. And those were the three people I was growing up with. That was it. From then on, I was growing up at the ice rink in Ukraine," she says. "I don't know of any other relatives on my mother's side."

She saw her father for the first and last time at her mother's funeral. But she says she knows for a fact he is still alive. "My mom and her parents never discussed my father, so at that point in my life I thought, if we are not talking about him, then he must be a bad person. I have no idea really why he was never discussed," she explains. "I know that there are a lot of relatives on his side, but we never talked about them or saw them."

Dr. Lodato speculates that the reason Oksana has no contact with her father today stems from fear. "She never knew him, so I guess the difficulty is she is afraid of what she might find." Several years ago, she made some effort to contact relatives in Ukraine, but abandoned it quickly.

Despite their lack of communication, Baiul believes her father is aware of her accomplishments and resolve. "I think he knows what I've done, and I think he's very proud of me," she states.

As well he should be. "Oksana has made tremendous strides in recent years. Basically, she grew up, and she stopped being the self-centered little girl, and she began thinking of other people and the maturing process took over. She responded well to it," states Dr. Lodato. "If you tried to predict the future based on what has happened up to this point, her prognosis would be quite good."

"Sure, she made some bad choices. She was an instant celebrity, and you try and determine what happiness is. A lot of what has happened to her has to do with self-esteem," theorizes Brian Orser. "She's now engaged and seems so much happier. Often times it takes something like that to put life into perspective. Good for her!"

Assesses Oksana, "I've gone through lots of ups and downs in my life, but now I'm definitely happy and so stable. I've finally gotten to the point I was looking for since my mom passed away. It's a wonderful feeling."

---

[1] Kristy Kim, Channel 7 News, WHDH-TV in Boston

Gone With the Gold

10

"There is a system in the USFSA. Tara Lipinski upset the apple cart by beating Michelle Kwan (at the 1998 Olympics). She was the youngest. She was always the rebel kid, so to speak, and she always went to the beat of a different drummer."

– Mike Burg, Tara's agent from 1995-99

Gone With the Gold

With new Olympic gold in tow, Tara Lipinski fled to the professional ranks in April 1998, at the ripe old age of 15.

At 16, she joined *Stars on Ice*.

Two years later, she endured major hip surgery.

Today, at age 20, her skating appearances outside of the tour have dwindled as her attention turns to a second passion: acting.

Tara's tale is one of talent, ambition, determination and isolation. Ignored by the establishment, she made her own way and hasn't looked back.

It all started rather inauspiciously when the then–roller skater took to the ice for the first time at the age of six.

"She was pathetic, really bad! Her ankles were going in, and she couldn't do anything," jokes Pat Lipinski, Tara's mother. "I turned to Jack (Tara's father) and said, 'Compare this to how she roller skates.'"

Tara's parents were ready to give it up, but Tara wasn't. Jack and Pat took their skates off and headed for the rink's café, and Tara kept plugging away at the public session. She had a big surprise for Mom and Dad when they returned an hour later. She had already mastered the basic waltz jump.

"She took what she knew on roller skates and was doing it on the ice," says Jack.

Recalls Pat, "Her legs were straight and everything was good, and she had this big smile on her face. And she said, 'Mom, when can I start lessons?'"

The answer was, right away.

"I just loved it so much! It progressed so quickly, and I didn't even realize how it happened," offers Tara. "First, I'm going to just take one lesson a week, because it will be fun. And then the coach is like, 'Why don't you just do this one competition?' And then you win that one competition, and then you keep going and going and going.

"As I got better, I think that's when I started to realize about the Olympics, and that became a cool dream."

The skating community and public took notice of Tara in 1994 when she won the Olympic Festival at age 12. While thrilled for their daughter, the subsequent press attention was more than the Lipinskis were prepared for.

"All of a sudden she was the darling of the media. Someone we know taped the broadcast. We heard this comment and that comment. They criticized her training three hours a day. Then they started talking about burnout," recalls Jack. "I looked at Pat and said, 'Oh, my God, the media loves her, and this thing isn't a week old and they're already looking for things to pick on!'"

"It was such a shock. I didn't know much about ice skating. I was used to roller skating where we went to parties and all the parents were together and we really had fun. So I wasn't prepared for any of this," explains Pat.

"I got a really funny feeling in my stomach. Jack and I went into this really naïve. Little did I know that that was my first media comment of the next five million to come that would be basically negative."

By the time the U.S. National Championships rolled around in 1995, the Tara media watch was in full court press. Entering the Junior Women's event, Tara was the hands-down favorite. But the crown went to little-known Sydne Vogel of Alaska. It was then that the whispering began—much of it from respected USFSA judges and officials. "Tara's too tiny." "Her jumps are too small." "Tara cheats her lutz jump." It was a pattern that would haunt the Lipinskis over the next few years as their daughter continued to quickly climb the skating ladder.

In 1996, Tara surprised everyone, including herself, when, at age 13, she made the senior U.S. World Team.

"I'd just changed coaches, my whole life was kind of up in the air, I was moving to Detroit and I was so young. I did well at Junior Nationals the year before, but I was second. I was just on my way, I thought, like any normal skater at that level," reasons Tara. "Then all of a sudden I came in third at Senior Nationals, and it was a real shock. Getting to Worlds hadn't even crossed my mind."

Skating at the 1996 World Championships in Edmonton, Canada, served as a real wake-up call for the then–13-year-old. "When I stepped onto the ice there, that's when I realized, *Oh my gosh, I'm playing with the big girls now*, and everything became more of a reality," says Tara.

It was immediately after this competition, Pat pinpoints, that the media's remarks about her daughter really took a turn for the worse.

"It got bad the day after Worlds. I was in a taxicab coming home from the airport. The driver knew us because he used to always pick us up, so he had all the newspapers. Tara and I hadn't seen them yet. I remember looking at one of the Detroit papers, and they were just going at Tara, her age and her [lack of] artistry. It just wasn't right," she contends.

"People really resented her age. All of a sudden people figured we were driving everything down in the sport, so everyone's now going to look like a tiny little gymnast or whatever," quips Jack.

While her parents have painful memories of this time, Tara's recollection is more tempered.

"Of course, I was always the little one, and it's always hard being the newcomer. You're not as accepted as others who have been around longer. So I had to deal with that," she admits. "I just kept skating. In hindsight, I see I was in my own little world."

As Pat and Jack's doubts and concerns about Tara's involvement in skating grew, it was their daughter's tremendous motivation that pulled everyone together. It was a particularly difficult situation for Pat. The homemaker had previously shuttled Tara back and forth to train in Delaware, and now she had moved to Detroit so that Tara could train with renowned coach Richard Callaghan. Jack stayed in Texas, where they had settled several years before.

"In the beginning, when all of this started with the media, it was really hard on Tara. She had to work hard to take care of me and keep me happy—to keep me in Delaware and Detroit. I had already reached the end of my rope by that point, because I didn't like what I was seeing," confesses Pat.

"Tara would beg me to keep skating. She had to totally love skating to get us though it, and she absolutely did."

The main reason for Tara and Pat's trek to Michigan was that coach Richard Callaghan, who still guides the career of six-time U.S. Men's Champion Todd Eldredge, was to work on Tara's much-criticized lutz jump.

It was a move that appeared to pay off nicely in competition, but the Lipinskis contend that it was far from a cordial relationship.

"It was strictly a business proposition. When Richard was on the ice with Tara, it was viewed as time for pay, and that was it," insists Jack. "There was never anything welcoming about it. I don't think Tara ever had a meal with him."

Pat says, "They never really had a talk. She never, ever had an upbeat talk with him. She never had anything. And I will swear to that!"

The Lipinskis say the only real attention Tara received at the Detroit Figure Skating Club came from assistant coach Craig Maurizi. Maurizi "made lessons fun for Tara," says Pat, but she doesn't believe he was always allowed to instruct her daughter. Tara also maintained contact with Megan Faulkner, who coached her back home in Sugar Land, Texas.

Pat adds that there were occasions in Detroit when Tara didn't even get a lesson. "If there were any problems with any other skaters, maybe that day she didn't get a lesson," Pat contends.

"It hurt Tara, because she saw other people with their coaches all the time. Everybody had their coach with them, and she'd see them talking and sitting with them, having a pep talk with them or walking with them in the streets when we'd be away for an international event. But Tara was always just with me," says Pat.

"It's OK to be with your Mom all the time, but not when you're that level of a competitor. You do need a high level coach. Mom needs to go away, and a coach needs to come in and fire you up," she assesses.

"There were so many times I was so frightened, because I was going through probably what all the other coaches were going through with their students, and I was going through it with Tara. And I'm not a coach, and I didn't know what to do!

"She'd come to me and say, 'I'm scared Mommy' or 'I don't think I can skate tonight' or 'How do I do this Mom?' And I didn't want to tell her to go to her coach, because it wasn't during a lesson."

Pat and Jack feel Callaghan didn't realize at all the skater he had in Tara. "It wasn't her time yet. Her time would come. It was Todd's time. I understand that. I'm the first to understand, too, that Richard was close to Todd, because he taught Todd since Todd was a baby," states Pat. "So you don't just come in from another state and think, *OK, now we're here.* But you really can't, at the level Tara was at—the Olympic level—you can't just go on a 40-minute lesson a day."

Richard Callaghan paints a decidedly different picture of his time with Tara. "I've always tried to coach the same no matter who the skater is or what level they are at," he says. "I feel that I have always been equal with my skaters. But you know, sometimes people perceive things differently. It's that simple."

The Lipinskis believe Tara's ultimate skating success largely came about due to the amazing focus that Tara and Pat poured into it, not due to outside forces.

"Jack had to work, because unbelievable bills had to be paid, plus he was thousands of miles away. So 'Team Tara' basically boiled down to Tara and myself. And I'm the first one to admit I think there were better ways to teach Tara how to handle pressure and things like that," offers Pat. "I am not a skater. I am not a coach. I didn't know what to do with a skater at that level. And I did my best. I held her while she cried more times than anyone will ever know. I gave her more pep talks than anyone will ever know."

Tara would come to need these discussions with her mother more and more.

Not even after the 1996–97 season, in which she won the U.S. Nationals, the Grand Prix Final and the World Championships, did Tara feel support from her own skating federation.

"I started to think that I had a huge chance at the Olympics, but it's hard, especially in a big association like that. The other skaters had been in it for a while. They didn't just come on the scene like I did. To me, at the time, I was working 10 hours a day at the rink just like everyone else, and the USFSA didn't see that. That was a hard thing," confesses Tara.

"Michelle [Kwan] was more established in the skating world, and she had a lot of fans. I was always the one the USFSA would say, 'We'll hold on to her for later.' That was hard for my confidence level, because I didn't have that support."

"I don't think people realized that Tara really was a phenom. We really hadn't seen anything like that before. She was that one in a million that comes through," declares Pat.

The Lipinskis can't recall the USFSA making an outreach of any kind. "They never really dealt with us. Basically, we never had communication with them," states Pat. "At the time, I didn't think they ever talked to anybody else. Back then nobody ever told me different."

A request for comment from the USFSA was not answered.

It was a much more welcoming sight on the international scene. "None of our local politics were involved. And overall, they judged what they saw, not what they wanted to see," declares Jack.

"I still think they wanted Tara to pay her dues a little bit longer, too, but if she skated clean, they gave it to her," says Pat. "I felt comfortable with the international judges. They were always nice to us. They might come over and say something to Tara that was always encouraging to us.

"We just did our best. We put skates on our daughter, and we put her on the ice. And we fought for what we wanted, for what we thought was right for her."

In the final analysis, though, Tara believes the lack of support from the USFSA didn't matter. "I had my parents, and I had my own drive."

It was this burning desire that got Tara through the battles during the Olympic season.

This included a difficult performance at the 1998 U.S. National Championships, where she took a hard fall in the short program and lost her national title to Michelle, who received a block of 6.0s from the judges.

"I was having problems with injuries and dealing with the pressure, because I'd just lost my national title, and I was really upset. I felt like no one thought I could do it. I would see in the newspaper, 'Tara can do a quad and she still won't win.' That kind of took its toll on me, and I struggled with that leading up to the Olympics," recalls Tara.

Undeniably, Michelle was the pre-ordained winner and the media favorite. "The bottom line of the articles was unfair, because it was a story where there was only one skater and everybody else is secondary. The fact of the matter is, it's a sport, and you're supposed to win based on what you put out at that moment in time," states Jack. "All of the stuff about Tara being a jumping bean and having no artistry was really annoying. Like I said in an interview then, 'If they want it to be ballet, why don't they simply call it ballet?'"

The Lipinskis always felt the Michelle versus Tara rivalry was pure media hype. "After Tara won Nationals (in 1997), I was reading one of the news magazines. It was like a boxing card. There was a picture of Michelle and a picture of Tara, what one does and what that one does. I remember telling Pat, 'Hold on to your hat, the media is going to turn this into a frenzy.' And they did. I'm sure all the girls wanted to do was win the Olympics," says Jack.

"It was one thing to turn it into the frenzy that they did. It's another thing not to realize they're dealing with a 15-year-old girl who was really working so hard to be the best skater she could possibly be, and she was doing the best she could with what she had—which was basically nothing. Not in terms of her talent, but she just didn't have a team," affirms Pat.

Leading the onslaught of criticism of Tara in the press was well-known journalist Christine Brennan, formerly with the *Washington Post* and now of *USA Today*.

"To ridicule someone and to diminish their titles because Christine happened to really like Michelle Kwan, I think is unfair and cruel to do to a young girl," declares Scott Hamilton. "It's a shame. I think that Christine hurt Tara publicly and personally.

"When you have young girls—15, 16, 17—that's a hard age. You're pretty much in the middle of being a child and an adult, and you have to go through that people are calling you out publicly and people are starting to write nasty things about you on the Internet, because of what they read in a newspaper or something.

"It just fuels this fire that can undermine somebody's ability to really explore their competitive careers and their potential public popularity."

Brennan contends that criticism of Tara should be viewed as complimentary.

"I certainly know that, over the years, people in skating believe I have been critical of Tara. I'm aware. I have my eyes open. But I think so much of that relates to my criticism of her turning professional right after the 1998 Olympics. It's important to note that that criticism—every time I mentioned it—was only in the vein that I wanted to see her continue to push herself athletically and artistically," explains Brennan.

"I believed, as did many others, that the way to do that was to be in the Olympic-eligible division. It would have been magnificent to see Michelle and Tara go at it like Chris [Evert] and Martina [Navratilova] did in tennis. So that is the ultimate compliment that I can pay to Tara Lipinski. To construe that as my being negative toward her is simply incorrect."

The Lipinskis say that on numerous occasions Brennan wrote about arguments between Tara and Pat that were blown way out of proportion and had nothing to do with skating.

"It's annoying, because so many times when you're in the public eye you don't have time to go into a private corner and say, 'Oh, you're not doing your homework now?' It doesn't work that way," attests Pat.

Another time, Brennan wrote in a book published shortly after the 1998 Olympics that she had seen the Lipinski family arguing in the stands after a competition. "We're simply trying to make a family problem go away. Instead, she wrote something about us fighting because Tara came in second."

Pat's accusations surprised Brennan.

"I stand by every word in my book, *Edge of Glory*. Everything I've written—in that book and in my column for *USA Today*—no one has ever said that anything was incorrect. No one ever came to me," she states. "All of the materials from Pat Lipinski in *Edge of Glory* were on the record and tape recorded. And at no time since has any member of the Lipinski family told me I got something wrong.

"I sincerely thank the Lipinskis for the time that they gave me over the years with interviews. If they had or have concerns, they have my home phone number. They know how to reach me."

Furthermore, Brennan says her recent encounters with Tara have been very positive. "I've gotten to know Tara pretty well the last couple of years. We bump into each other at various things and get along fine," she says.

With the media storm around them, Pat says, not once did any member of the media try to talk to them for clarification.

"Oh, and I did want to talk! I think the press really knew that the true story they'd get from us wasn't going to sell. I always used to tell them, if you really want to know, please, I will tell you from the bottom of my heart. I will swear on a Bible for you. I will tell you the truth," Pat says. "And they looked at me and figured this was going to be a sad sob story, which they didn't want. The other story is much better."

The media had such an effect on the Lipinskis during the Olympic period that they elected not to publicly mention Tara's nagging back injury.

"It had already been released to the press about Michelle's injured foot. Tara was having problems before this happened. But then Tara got terribly worse where we should have probably said something, but because of bad timing and Michelle's announcement, we felt we couldn't say anything, because people would go, 'Oh, oh, oh, that's just the Lipinskis,'" explains Pat.

Adds Jack, "At this point the media was looking for anything. They were even picking on Tara's dress."

Pat decided she couldn't deal with any added stress. "I said. 'It'll hurt me so bad, because it's true. Tara's suffering, and we're in hospitals and having MRIs.' I was scared out of my mind.

"We used to try to help ourselves not get as upset by not saying anything at all. The less you said, the less you could get hurt. We kept it a secret, because we really didn't want to take the backlash of what would be said because of her back. I don't know to this day if we did the right thing."

It was a frustrating time. Tara was in pain, and doctor after doctor failed to diagnose the source of her back injury.

"Nobody could help us. They knew there were problems with her back. You just had to look at it to see. But they never could diagnose a hip problem," says Pat. This is the same hip injury that would ultimately require surgery two-and-a-half years down the road.

Somehow Tara was able to put everything behind her and give the performances of her young life when it mattered most. Not only that, but she truly enjoyed her Olympic experience, marching in the Opening and Closing ceremonies and mingling amongst the athletes from different nations. Michelle, on the other hand, chose to skip the Opening ceremonies, arrive in Nagano several days into the Olympics and resided in a hotel throughout the games.

"I knew that I wanted this Olympics, because I might not be around for the next one," explains Tara. "I just tried to go there and put everything aside. Finally, something just happened and I said, 'You know what, I don't care. I'm going to go out, and I'm going to skate and show everyone what I can do!'"

Tara insists winning was never about getting revenge. "Instead, it was more like, 'Ha, I did it, you see?' I had to prove it. It was total happiness. If you can accomplish your dream, and a big one such as that, it's just happiness inside."

It was also a feeling of relief, at least for Pat. "No one knows what my life was like that Olympic year," she proclaims. "There were so many times I would say something to Tara and it would go well. I just lucked out, because I prayed a lot before I said it. And she'd give me a big smile, and everything would be good. And then there were times I would say something and you'd see her stare at me, and I'd think, *Oh, I said the wrong thing.*

"She won just in time, because if she was 17 and 18, and we were still having to live like that, there's no way she would have done it. She would have been smart, and she would have known I made a mistake and thought, *Gee, I need a real coach.*"

Tara's victory over Michelle, though a clear one by a vote of six judges to three, did not endear her to the USFSA as the Lipinskis had hoped. In fact, the U.S. judge had voted to give Michelle the gold. "After Tara won, everybody was told to just, like, make believe it didn't happen," offers Pat.

In part, they blame a high-powered agent of another skater for Tara's blacklisting of sorts. "I heard him say once that over his dead body will Tara ever have anything. And he really meant it!" suggests Pat.

While some in skating may have wished Tara hadn't won Olympic gold, *Stars on Ice* creative director Sandra Bezic contends the victory was a gift to skating.

"I'm not saying that Sarah Hughes would not have happened without Tara winning the Olympics, but what Tara did when she won the Olympics was live the fairy tale that dreams do come true. All the Sarah Hughes' of the world looked at her victory and thought, *I can do it too*," explains Bezic.

"Tara did the Olympics right. She experienced the entire Olympics and gave it her all, instead of viewing it as more of a job. She reminded us of the Olympic dream with her innocence. That was an amazing thing."

Two months after the Olympics—during which time Tara skipped the 1998 World Championships—she announced she was turning professional. It was news many in the skating world didn't see coming. At the time, Tara said it was to be with, and for, her family. Her parents had spent much of the prior few years in separate states: Jack at work in Texas and Pat where Tara trained. It was too much of a strain on the family, and Tara wanted to make it better.

But she now admits the main reason she left the eligible ranks was injury. "It was definitely my hip, though I really didn't say that at the time," Tara says. "There was a culmination of things: the hip, living away from home and realizing that my family was split up. And just that I'd accomplished what I wanted to, and even though people thought I could have stayed in longer, I knew I couldn't. My hip wouldn't hold up and I didn't want to be in the next Olympics and have to quit and watch everyone else keep skating for the rest of their lives."

Tara's then-agent Mike Burg says he fully presented the pros and cons of the situation to his client.

"The option was, if you stay eligible, you are going to be facing Michelle and the other young guns every day. That is just what competition is about. That will keep you in the limelight. If you turn pro, you will have a very comfortable living, but you will fall out of the limelight. And it was clearly their decision," he says.

"I think at the end of the day the rivalry that the media and everyone had built up between her and Michelle was so intense. She was hurting physically all year long. I think finally it was just kind of a relief to say, I just want to enjoy myself, because it was great, but getting there was an incredibly difficult battle politically and otherwise."

Burg reports Tara did very well financially right before and after the Olympics, so income didn't play a factor. "Sure, she would have sustained a higher level had she stayed eligible, but that wasn't the issue," he says. "At this point, she had gotten enough money to last her forever. It was a lifestyle question."

Comfortable with her eligible skating behind her, Tara focused on touring and exploring her creative horizons. She did *Champions on Ice* in the summer of 1998 and made the jump to *Stars on Ice* that fall.

The decision to switch tours was Pat's idea. "I love *Champions on Ice*, but at the time I thought, *I have a 15-year-old, and she's turned pro. Now what is she going to do?* Every day she's just going to go and do her program, and that would be it. And I thought to myself, she's so young. Maybe she still needs to be at the bottom of the pack. And she still has to grow. That's all I wanted for her, and I thought of Scott Hamilton, who was my idol. There's somebody who could teach her," she explains.

"I'll put her in *Stars on Ice*, and he's going to show her the ropes. It will take years, but that's OK. I don't care if it takes 10 years. She is going to learn to be a true entertainer. It's like a Broadway show, and I wanted Tara to do group numbers, because I knew she loved them from her roller skating days. And I thought, this kid's going to love this, because she's in her element. She'll be doing group numbers, and she won't even know that she's learning from Scott."

Good intentions aside, it hasn't been quite the experience the Lipinskis had hoped for Tara. She's found little camaraderie with the *Stars on Ice* cast, except for Kurt Browning.

"The only thing I can say without getting Tara in trouble is that Tara was isolated. Isolation kills you. Isolation makes you not want to live or be a part of the tour or do anything," reveals Pat. "It's sad, because they expected her to work as hard as they did.

But if you work that hard, where do you get your energy? Where do you let your energy go at night? Would anybody want to work that hard all day long and then go up to a room and sit and stare at a wall?"

Adds Jack, "She was so young [that] they totally ignored her. Their relationships were made years ago, and there was no room for anyone else."

People associated with the tour, who prefer not to be identified, say Tara often demanded attention. There are also complaints that at times she did not treat her fellow skaters with respect.

"What she just couldn't understand was that in *Champions* she was even younger, and they always included her. If they went someplace, Tara went with them. She was like their little sister," shares Pat. "I remember calling Tara the summer she was on the tour after the Olympics, and her saying she could never talk to me. I remember feeling kind of bad for myself, because she didn't have time for me. Little did I know how happy she was back then. And how happy I should have been because she was so happy. She was having so much fun.

"The worst thing is that I took my daughter from one place, where she was in heaven, and thought I was doing such a good thing for her," says Pat. "I am in awe right now of Tom Collins, because now I know what he did for Tara. He really cares about his skaters and takes tremendous care of them."

Tara, however, contends that she enjoyed that first year in *Stars on Ice*.

One thing is for certain: she loves life on the road. "Touring is my dream job in skating," she says. "I'm happy with that. Someday my own tour would be cool! You can't get a better feeling than when you're standing out there and all these thousands of people are just watching you. You have this chance to touch them and make them feel something when you're skating."

In the last four years, Tara feels she's grown immensely as a performer. "I feel, as an amateur, I didn't even know what to do. I think that's the big thing about turning pro, you finally realize what performing is all about. You thought you knew as an amateur, but you really didn't. You just learn more every year," she explains.

Tara hopes to have the same evolution as she works on another aspiration: establishing herself as an actress.

The seriousness of this pursuit was received loud and clear when, in December 2001, she left agent Gary Swain and IMG for the legendary William Morris Agency, renowned in entertainment circles.

"I wanted to take my career in a different direction. I love *Stars on Ice*, but I'm really getting into acting. I've found out you have to take it seriously. I want to skate, but I'm going to pursue acting. These people who are working with me are not just skating. It's mostly about everything else that I'm doing. I want to expand myself into other areas," explains Tara.

Her equating acting with skating in terms of priority has baffled or annoyed some in the sport. But others, like Sarah Hughes' coach, Robin Wagner, believe people should just mind their own business.

"I think it is a shame the negative comments that have gone on about Tara, because I think we too often judge what is right for somebody. I assume she is very happy," Wagner states. "True, maybe she hasn't gone on in the skating community [as expected], but who are we to really judge whether she should be an actress or not?"

Ironically, Tara's skating had a hand in her being bitten by the acting bug.

"I always loved movies. Then I started to do a few of the sitcoms, just walk-ons. And when I got on tour with *Stars on Ice*, it was more about acting on ice. I realized, this is cool, and I loved it!"

Tara has appeared on the CBS prime-time drama *Touched by an Angel* and the soap opera *The Young and the Restless*. There have also been appearances in TV movies, such as *Ice Angel*. In the summer of 2001, Tara worked on an independent film called *Metro Chase*, and recently had meetings about appearing on several television shows.

Tara says she doesn't have a favorite type of role. "I really like playing either the good girl or the more controversial girl. Whatever comes up I seem to enjoy.

"My goal is to cross over and show people that I'm not just an athlete playing at acting," she states. "I really study and work hard. I've gotten good responses."

Looking to the future, Tara sees herself immersed in both skating and acting.

"I want to skate as long as I can. I love touring and bringing those fans to me, and it's just incredible. But I also love acting. It takes a long time in acting to get established, so I hope in the next couple of years I can work my way there."

"She's of the generation that's wanting to be a star," says Rosalynn Sumners. "Every teenager wants to be Britney Spears, and Tara has a platform to do it. I see Tara as more of a real crossover into entertainment. She has that attitude and mentality, which is very cool."

Choreographer Lea Ann Miller, who worked with Tara for three years, believes she has that certain something. "She's got that aura and that look about her. She's got that star quality ... what all the young girls try to be. I watch the way she puts herself together. If she does anything in Hollywood with acting, she will be fabulous at it."

Today Tara indeed feels comfortable with the roads she has chosen. She says she has endured criticism because of her close ties with her parents, but she readily accepts their guidance. "That's the way I feel it should be," she states. "I trust them more than anyone. We have this great relationship, and it makes me feel better when I get their opinions, even though I now make all my own decisions.

"My parents are also a huge grounding system for me, and I have my best friend (former U.S. pair skater Erin Elbe) with me all the time, so I have my life where I can just be a teenager. I'm doing a tour. I'm trying to act. I'm doing lots of charity work as a spokesperson. I feel like since I have these opportunities, and as long as I'm having fun and enjoying them, then I should do them—so I am!"

Michelle Kwan, Inc.

"Skating fans tell me they feel like they know me. They do, because I've been doing this for so long out in front of them. They've seen me cry for good things and for bad things. They see a whole range of emotions and who I actually am."

– Michelle Kwan,
four-time World Women's Champion,
six-time U.S. Champion,
Olympic silver and bronze medalist

Michelle Kwan, Inc.

In a sport defined by luminaries, Michelle Kwan is the guiding star.

Fans adore her.

Companies want her image linked with theirs.

And figure skating sees dollar signs.

A third-place finish in Salt Lake City behind fellow American Sarah Hughes, who won Olympic gold, didn't even make her light flicker. Today, it burns as brightly as ever.

"A lot of people think I won the Olympics," marvels Michelle.

Three weeks after the 2002 Olympic Winter Games, Michelle added to her vast list of commercial endorsements by signing a three-year contract with The Walt Disney Company to be a celebrity representative and spokesperson.

On the post Olympic *Champions on Ice* tour—which also

included Hughes—Michelle was clearly the one who received the loudest ovation. And while other skaters were introduced as Olympic, World or National medalists, Michelle was introduced simply as "America's Own."

"It makes me smile when they say my name and the audience starts clapping," she notes. "Some days when I am not feeling too well, it is just about skating for them, and performing makes me better. It feels good!"

Michelle sets the standard with the television networks, too. To have her skate in an event is viewed as a sure formula for success, to the point where ABC Sports—in addition to the over $100 million, 10-year contract with the USFSA—signed Michelle to a separate contract to guarantee her appearance at competitions.

In the last four years, Michelle has captured the corporate market like no other figure skater, with over 20 different ventures, from McDonald's and ESPN commercials, to a Hallmark snow globe, to multi-year deals with Chevrolet and now Disney. In 1999, she was the only female athlete named in the Top 10 Athletic Endorsers, as compiled by Burns Sports Celebrity Service.

Kwan says that her agent, Shep Goldberg, gets numerous requests from companies, but they follow simple criteria.

"First, I have got to believe in the product or believe in the company, and, of course, I just have to make sure it is the right thing for me and that I can represent it well and that I have time for it. I know that there are a lot of things out there, but you just have to be sure that it is right for you," Michelle explains.

"If I capitalized on everything that came my way, I would be a mess, mentally. Skating is my first love. Everything else is extra,"[1] she states.

Undeniably, though, Michelle is excited about her recent deal with Disney, which includes her appearing at their theme parks and doing radio, theatrical, video and voice-over work. This is Disney's most extensive agreement to date with any athlete.

In September, she worked on *Mulan 2*, a direct-to-video release slated for 2004, which is a sequel to her 1998 television special.

"The Disney specials were a lot of fun. A lot of skating, but a lot of creative ideas and things that you can't put in a regular skating program," she notes. "In general, Disney has been so wonderful. It has really let me branch out in a way that I never thought I would be able to. There have been so many opportunities. And I think there is more to come, so I am excited."

So is Disney, who didn't think of not signing Kwan after she again lost the Olympic gold.

"We never really even considered that. You just look at the type of person she is, the qualities she brings within her personality, her leadership, focus, commitment. Staying with something, staying committed to something. 'Don't let minor disappointments along the way keep you from your dreams, kids. Follow your dream.' It's about passion, and for me that's so much more,"[2] offers Mike Mendenhall, president of marketing and synergy for Walt Disney Studios.

"To us, she's a great role model for kids and teens. She truly has the right attitude, the right ethics, the right personality. She's contemporary. She's relevant,"[3] he contends.

Chevrolet also feels the same.

"To be honest, we got a lot of questions after the Olympics," said Dianne Harper, a promotional manager for Chevrolet. "Like, 'She didn't win the gold medal, so....' And I would say, 'Yeah, and your point?'

"It doesn't matter. It's who she is, and her value to us doesn't decrease because she doesn't have a gold medal. The original reasons we liked Michelle hold up today,"[4] explains Harper.

In the months following the Salt Lake Winter Games, Michelle won the Teen Choice and Nickelodeon Kids' Choice Awards for favorite female athlete. The contestants at the 2002 Miss Teen USA pageant gave her the title of most admired athlete.

So what is it about Michelle that makes her so popular and so bankable?

Perseverance and dignity are near the top.

"Michelle's relationship with the public has developed over the years," offers Hughes' coach, Robin Wagner. "She has been a humble, gracious sportsperson—win or lose. She has always come out with a very positive attitude, which I think people like to see in an athlete."

"I think it's because of her actions in Nagano (site of the 1998 Winter Olympics, where she finished second behind fellow American Tara Lipinski in a close battle), and that she didn't win. And that she didn't win this time, yet she handled it with grace," offers Brian Boitano.

After all, figure skating is a sport, and if everyone skated perfectly all the time, why would anyone watch? So the fact that Michelle does falter on the ice from time to time makes her all the more human and endearing.

"The audience also knows that she's an Olympic gold medalist, without getting that gold medal. It's not like she isn't the best in the world, or hasn't been at some time the best in the world," Brian reasons.

"They just see the potential, they see who she's become and how she's matured. You can tell that she loves skating."

"Skating means so much to me in the long run," Michelle says. "The Olympic gold, if you can achieve it, great. If you can win, that is great. There is one person every four years.

"If I don't ever win, it is OK," she adds. "I am OK with it. But for my own sake, skating has brought so much to me."

Says USFSA President Phyllis Howard, "Michelle has been such a recognizable name, and her grace on the ice has translated into the way she has conducted herself off the ice too."

Choreographer Lori Nichol, who worked with Michelle from 1993 to 2001, feels there is a bit of mystery with her that pulls people in.

"I've always felt that there's something deep within Michelle that isn't easy to put one simple description to," she says.

"Plus, her edge quality and her body lines are fantastic, and I think we are drawn to her, because she really changed a lot of how women skate in the world today."

But perhaps the biggest catalyst for "Kwanmania" is her familiarity. In the spotlight, Michelle has blossomed from a scrawny, pig-tailed girl to a 22-year-old lady.

"I hope people enjoy my skating, and I can be a part of everyone's lives, touch them in my four minutes on the ice. I hope I have [made] and that I make life a little more enjoyable," she says.

Maybe it's the seeping effect. Nichol says a word she used a lot in her early days of working with Michelle was "ooze."

"I chose the word 'ooze' to help her understand the tension that can be within movement and to help with transitions from one move to the next—to get that feeling within the knee bend and create the quality of edge we were looking for," she says. "That one word really dictated a lot of what we did."

The audiences have felt that flowing connection with Michelle and readily channel their energies in her direction. From the Olympic exhibition to the *Champions on Ice* tour, it seemed people everywhere were on a mission to let her know they're still with her all the way.

"It's more a reassurance, not like a pity," she says. "Reassurance like, 'Hey, you know, it doesn't matter. Life's not perfect,' kind of attitude…. They realize the pain. That's the wrong word. That that's the way life goes sometimes. You have to kind of shrug your shoulders and move on,"[5] Michelle says.

"That means a lot. For me, it feels sometimes like it would have made a difference (if she had won Olympic gold). People would have looked at me a little different. Then again, it's hard to say what it's like, because I've only known one thing, and that's not having it,"[6] she assesses.

When it's all said and done, Michelle finds her position in figure skating and with the public pretty incredible.

"I wish I could tell you what made me, but I don't know," she states. "It's amazing!"

Michelle even likes that people are interested her in personal life. "It makes me feel really good about myself, because it is not just about my skating, but more as a human being. I appreciate that," she says. Despite that declaration, she has never publicly spoken about her boyfriend, hockey player Brad Ference, a defenseman with the Florida Panthers of the NHL.

"There have to be limitations, and sometimes I feel people don't recognize limitations," she says. "Of course, you want to be open and tell the truth, but when it comes to my personal life and not skating, that's a little different.

"People don't know what happened behind the scenes," she continues. "I understand that people are curious. I get curious too, but come on."

Michelle emphasizes she is keenly aware that children and teens look up to her. She only wishes every athlete understood this.

"I hear other athletes say, 'I don't want to be a role model.' But you are, because you're in the spotlight. You have to be responsible when kids look up to you. Be aware of that," she declares.

While Kwan, the enterprise, and Kwan, the personality, came through last season with flying colors, Kwan, the competitive skater, endured her share of stumbles—arguably all of her own doing.

"I would say, clearly, I am my worst enemy, for sure," she replies, when asked who her most fierce competitor has been. "I have never been really competitive with the girls. I look after myself. You just do your own thing."

In June 2001, Michelle ended her eight-year collaboration with Lori Nichol and replaced her with Sarah Kawahara, with whom Kwan had worked on her ABC Disney specials. Then, on the eve of the Skate America competition in October, she dismissed Frank Carroll, who had coached her for a decade.

A year earlier, in the July/August 2000 issue of *International Figure Skating* magazine, Michelle lavished praise on both Nichol and Carroll and insisted they were in it together for the long haul.

"A lot of people change choreographers because they want to change the look," she explained then. "But I think Lori's evolving with me. Some choreographers may like a certain style, and that's how it is. I think that's why Lori and I work so well together."

As for Carroll, Michelle said, "He knows me so well on the ice. I can't imagine having another coach." In fact, that has thus far been true. After parting with Carroll, she didn't retain another coach for nearly a year.

According to Nichol, the end of her relationship with Michelle didn't come as a shock. "I'm amazed we worked together as exclusively as we did for as long as we did," she declares.

News of Carroll's ousting was a different story.

"Letting the choreographer go is one thing," said Nichol in February before the Olympics. "But the coach!"[7]

In several interviews since her dismissal, Nichol has revealed that tension in the Kwan camp had been building up for several years. Specifically, since Michelle tested the waters outside of skating and enrolled in UCLA in 1999.

"I certainly couldn't begrudge her wanting to go to school, but it was frustrating," Nichol states. "We were ready to take her further, and she had less time for skating than ever before."[8]

But Michelle says those school days only enhanced her performing abilities, because they broadened her horizons and heightened her awareness.

"UCLA has been amazing," she says. "They are not worried about my being able to jump, to spin, do revolutions. It has really put a lot into perspective."

With that perspective came the decision to move into new skating territory.

"It's nothing against Frank or Lori. You have to make decisions that are in the best interest for you," offered Michelle at the press conference announcing her split with Carroll. "I want to have the space so I can get myself together again.

"I've been doing this a long time," she further explained. "The passion is still there, but sometimes you just have to—it's sort of like splashing more flavor and more ingredients into it."

Michelle insisted there wasn't a fight that brought about her dismissal of Carroll and that she had thought intently about the decision for months.

"As I've gotten older, it seems, I've gotten more independent. As the relationship evolves, I think I've become stronger and think for myself. That's all I can say," she said, somewhat cryptically.

Later on, however, she gave a little more insight to

International Figure Skating magazine in the January/February 2002 issue. "The whole last month before I made the decision was hard. I know that Frank wants to help me be the best skater I can be," she said. "But there are a few things you just have different opinions about. And you start to drift away. You have to make the right decisions for yourself."

Requests to talk to Carroll about Michelle for *Frozen Assets* were ignored. However, he did speak about the split at a press conference last October.

"The only real explanation I've had from Michelle about this is that she really has a strong, strong feeling that she needs to do this by herself," shared an admittedly shocked Carroll.

"That she has to be strong enough to get out there and lay it on the line and put it on the line herself, without depending on me or depending on her father or depending on any outside influence.

"I feel like there's something going on in her head, and she can't seem to explain it," he stated.

Carroll was clearly blindsided by the news.

"I didn't expect it. I thought that there was nothing we couldn't work through. I love Michelle Kwan terribly," he announced. "We've spent a lot of time together, ever since she was a little girl. In the future, I would do whatever I can to help her and support her."

The media establishment—the same one who built Kwan up and favored her over Tara Lipinski and all other U.S. women—simply couldn't get over what Kwan had done. They believed there had to be something more to it.

"The media think there's something that went on between Frank and me that I haven't told," says Michelle. "They think there is something I'm keeping a secret. There's nothing."

"I thought those people knew me. But in some ways, I don't

think they know the real me. I'm just a normal person."

The harshness of the media criticism, particularly in the wake of her close defeat of Sarah Hughes at Skate America, hit Michelle like a slap in the face.

"You get shocked sometimes," she acknowledges. "This season, my mouth has dropped open thinking, *That was the rudest thing I've heard in my life. You expect me to answer that? What gives you the power to treat people like that?* Sometimes it's really painful."

In the end, it was Michelle's father, Danny Kwan, who stood at the boards while she skated at both Nationals and the Olympics and sat next to her in the kiss & cry area as she awaited her marks.

"It was pretty interesting, because I didn't know how he would handle himself in front of everybody, especially because he has always been a nervous parent walking around the arena," Michelle admits.

"Sometimes he hasn't even watched me skate at an event, so for him to actually be right by my side, staring at me right before at the most important event in my life—it was special. I was very impressed."

When Michelle faltered again on the Olympic stage, everyone wondered if the pressure got to her. Or, more specifically, if it was hard to jump with the media on your back and if that had caused her to crack.

"I think Michelle Kwan put the pressure on herself. You can't blame the media," declares 1994 Olympic Women's silver medalist Nancy Kerrigan, who knows a thing or two about media pressure. She also knows Kwan, having toured with her for several years in *Champions on Ice.*

"She was 12 years old when she told me she wanted to win

three Olympic gold medals. So it was in her head, she wanted to have these records. She had been to the other Olympics, didn't win a gold, so she had that pressure from herself," states Nancy.

"Michelle is a pretty stable young woman to deal with things in the media. She's very good with the press, it seems. With the skating, she expected a lot of herself, which she had a right to, she's very good. She's got all the records."

Kristi Yamaguchi concurs.

"I definitely think there is a lot of pressure. But it's hard to blame the media, because they always want a heroine and a hero. You look at [Olympic short track speed skater] Apolo Anton Ohno, who had a lot of media attention, too. There's so much pressure," says Kristi.

"Obviously, in the last two Olympics, it was the underdog [in the women's event] who came in and surprised everyone. I think they didn't quite feel the pressure. You can't blame the media, though, because the public wants more of Michelle.

"She was everyone's hope. We wanted to see everything that was going on in her mind and how she was preparing. I guess sometimes it just affects them too much."

Scott Hamilton, on the other hand, thinks Michelle was exploited by all those wanting a piece of her.

"Michelle was really the star. She was everything they had to sell. The Russian skaters are winning everything else, and you've got Michelle Kwan as your champion. You've got this television contract where you've got to put something on the air every single week. You can't go many weeks without Michelle, because what else are you selling? But if you do that too much, if you put Michelle under too much, then people are getting used to it, and that hurts her," maintains Scott.

"You need to come and go, you need to do different things, you need to be respectful and attentive to the way you expose your-self," he continues. "Sometimes I really felt like Michelle was put in a position where she had to go out there all the time.

"It's nice to be wanted, it's nice to be respected and adored. But I just think there's only so much you can do before you burn your-self out. I was always worried that her associations were going to burn Michelle out."

Nancy's husband and manager, Jerry Solomon, offers yet anoth-er take. He thinks even the question of Michelle buckling under the pressure is an unfair one. "But for a great performance by Tara Lipinski and a spectacular, historic performance by Sarah Hughes, she would have won," he rationalizes.

Tai Babilonia feels Michelle should be applauded for her resolve. "My hat goes off to her. Year after year, she has kept put-ting herself through this, and I don't know how she does it. She obviously loves it and is obsessed with it. She has wanted more and more and more. I give her a lot of credit," she offers.

Michelle says she owes much of her fortitude and inner strength to traits her family instilled. "I'm very close to them. But of course, it all happens from within you, too. To last long, you have to be able to stay focused," she explains. "You have to take one thing at a time."

Of all her achievements—seven World medals, four of them gold, and 10 U.S. National medals, six of them gold—Michelle says her greatest satisfaction is skating on the *Champions on Ice* tour. "I consider being on that tour a real accomplishment. It's very sat-isfying to be able to travel around the United States and see cities I would otherwise probably not see. Plus, we're treated very well on the tour," she says.

"Skating has been very good to me. I have been very fortunate to be able to travel to Japan, to Paris and see Versailles. That alone has been wonderful."

Perhaps her love of *Champions on Ice* comes back to that all-important family dynamic.

"We're the Collins family, and that's the Kwan family. We're very family oriented," says *Champions on Ice* executive producer Tom Collins. "I have never questioned her loyalty, I never even think about it. I know the Kwan family, and they know I've been very, very, very loyal to them through the years. So it's a mutual admiration society."

Her commitments on and off the ice keep her on the go, which she loves. "I know once I'm home for three days and do nothing, I'm like, *Let's go again.* It's school, skating and touring. I have to keep myself busy," Michelle states.

"I'm young and have so much energy. I have to do something. I'll have time to relax—when I get older and retire!"

Michelle says she is at a stage where she is asserting more control over her life.

"Before, I had my parents to look after my schedule and stuff, but now I am making my own decisions, and I have to be very, very picky, because I don't want to be too exhausted. I want to have my own personal time to do the things that matter to me, like be with my family," she relates.

"There are a lot of opportunities. It's very nice to have those options, but those decisions are tough. So many doors are open, you don't know which is the right one, and it's pretty scary for me. I'm 22, and I'm making life-altering decisions,"[9] shares Michelle.

She has, however, already faced down her Olympic demon. "My parents always told me never to live with regret, and I think I have done a pretty good job so far," she says.

It appears she will be going light with competitions this year, but she says, "I am not sure if I am ready to hang up my boots and blades. It is not like I have to define my eligibility right now. So I have to wait and see, you know. What I feel like is I don't want to shut all the doors, and there is no reason to."

She has been called the greatest female skater ever by many in the sport. How does Michelle envision her legacy?

"I always ask myself, What do I want people to remember?" she states. "I want something other than the sport ... more of an emotion. Not somebody who did so many triples. It's all too technical. It's more about whatever happiness I brought to them at a certain moment."

And what does Michelle see herself doing five to 10 years from now? "Definitely married and having kids," she notes. "Career-wise, I have no idea. Right now, it is making lots of twists and turns. But I'm ready for it."

[1] Bruce Horowitz, February 2000, *USA Today*

[2, 3, 4, 5, 6, 9] Helene Elliott, September 17, 2002, "Good as Gold," *The Los Angeles Times*

[7, 8] Russell Scott Smith, February 2002, "Withering Queen?" *Sports Illustrated Women*

Conflict

12

"No question, Jamie and David were the better pair that night. An injustice was done. It was recognized, and everybody ultimately got what they deserved—sort of. When people talk to me about Jamie and David they go, 'That's the team that got second at the Olympics, but got a gold medal after all.' Figure skating will never be the same. It has put a blemish on our sport."

– Lloyd Eisler, two-time
Olympic Pair bronze medalist

Conflict

What an unbelievable seven days in February.
The controversial pair figure skating result dominated the 2002 Olympic Winter Games and engrossed North America. Experts scoffed at the decision, and fans were left scratching their heads.

Seemingly, nobody could understand how Canadians Jamie Salé & David Pelletier lost the pair gold medal to Russians Elena Berezhnaya & Anton Sikharulidze. Jamie and David played out their *Love Story* program to perfection, while Anton had a slight bobble on the landing of a double axel jump.

Instantly, the scandal coined "Skategate" took on a life of its own.

It started as a media battle.

The zealous, decisive commentary of NBC's Scott Hamilton

cued all the press and public that something was "rotten in Denmark." From television networks to national magazines and newspapers, everyone got in on the act.

Then it became an internal investigation for the ISU.

French judge Marie-Reine Le Gougne broke down in a hotel lobby and confessed to then-chairwoman of the ISU Figure Skating Technical Committee Sally Stapleford that she was pressured by her federation president, Didier Gailhaguet, to vote for the Russian team.

It turned into a crusade for Skate Canada and the Canadian Olympic Association, which had not seen Olympic figure skating gold in over four decades. Feeling unjustly denied, they fought to the end for Jamie and David.

Finally, it was an embarrassing and unbearable headache for the International Olympic Committee (IOC). A week's worth of media barrage, with no signs of abatement, and the ISU dragging its feet forced the IOC to step in and insist the matter be resolved. The answer: a second gold medal awarded to the Canadians.

Over 2,500 other athletes from 78 nations in 11 sports had been hopelessly overshadowed. The legitimacy, and even existence, of figure skating had been brought into question.

The cat was let out of the bag for millions and millions to see. Deals and biases abound in the sport, and its subjective nature leaves the door wide open for such activity.

After the big blow in Salt Lake, the subsequent World Championships in Nagano, Japan, was like kicking someone already down.

The controversial awarding of the ice dancing bronze medal to Israelis Galit Chait & Sergey Sakhnovksy over Margarita Drobiazko & Povilas Vanagas of Lithuania sent 90 percent of the dance competitors over the edge. Irate, the dancers banded together and signed a petition protesting the result.

Away from the glare of the North American media and free to govern themselves—unlike in Salt Lake City where the IOC ruled the roost—the ISU ignored the protest.

The Olympic scandal, though, simply won't go away. At the end of July, another shoe dropped.

Reputed Russian mobster Alimzhan Tokhtakhounov was arrested in Italy for conspiring to fix the results of the pair and ice dance competitions. His single goal, allegedly, was to ensure Olympic gold for the French ice dancers Marina Anissina (who is Russian-born) & Gwendal Peizerat. Tokhtakhounov allegedly bartered with the Russian figure skating federation, using the pair competition as bait, pledging the vote of the French judge to Berezhnaya and Sikharulidze.

Based on information released by the FBI, which is undertaking the Tokhtakhounov investigation, speculation runs high that Anissina, to some degree, was aware of the plot.

Skating has certainly faced quite a series of curious circumstances in 2002. Thoughts on these predicaments run the gamut inside the skating community.

Firstly, who deserved to win—Jamie and David or Elena and Anton?

The majority agrees that Jamie and David were denied victory.

Leading the charge with Hamilton was NBC analyst Sandra Bezic, herself a former Canadian Pair Champion. "I don't think that there was anyone in that room, in that arena that night, that thought that Jamie and David shouldn't have won, except for the few judges," she says.

"It was really obvious that Jamie and David skated better that night. However, one of the first things that came to my mind was the track records of the skaters. Elena and Anton have been on

229

the scene longer and have a much bigger history in skating than Jamie and David, who started together four years ago. Sometimes that matters in skating," assesses Canadian Ice Dance champion Victor Kraatz.

"Jamie and David were definitely the best that night, and the judges messed it up for themselves, because they should have gotten it right in the first place," charges Brian Orser.

It wasn't just Jamie and David's countrymen who felt so strongly on their behalf. So, too, did Elena Bechke, herself once a skater under Tamara Moskvina, coach of Elena and Anton.

"I was watching it with my husband, and I turned to him and said, 'They lost it, Elena and Anton lost it with that mistake.' When the Canadians finished I was like, 'That's it, Elena and Anton are second,' because it was so obvious who won. The Canadians were so perfect and so precise. It was the perfect performance.

"I was so shocked when Elena and Anton were first. I couldn't believe it. They are beautiful, great skaters, but the Canadians deserved the gold medal," Bechke says.

Not everyone felt it was so clear cut. Choreographer and former U.S. pair skater Lea Ann Miller offers an explanation, one never legitimately addressed by the NBC commentators of the event.

"While Jamie and David skated fabulously, and for that Olympic moment probably deserved gold, I wasn't impressed they couldn't come up with something new for the Olympics," she says.

"Skating has always has been judged a little bit by the programs you've done, and you can have your own opinion about whether or not that's fair. If you're a judge, there's a creative energy you feel from a program. Sometimes skaters get 6.0s when something's not only great, but also fresh and new."

Jamie and David's *Love Story* was three years old. It brought the house down in Canada at the Grand Prix Final, their last international event prior to the Olympics. Buoyed by the response, the duo opted to use it instead of their new, well received and more demanding classic Rachmaninov free program they called *Orchid*.

Lori Nichol, the choreographer of both of these free programs, says the choice to use *Love Story* was an easy call at the time, refuses to look at the what-ifs and is annoyed with the second guessers.

"In the last year, we've gotten a lot of flack for doing a used program from before, which—if you could go back and wanted to get into statistics and look at how many people skated programs they'd used before, I think it would shut people up pretty quickly," she quips.

"With *Love Story* and the connection Jamie and David have with the audience, I strongly believe that there are just right pieces for people, and that was a right piece for them. Plus, in my view, I believe that David and Jamie had not skated *Orchid* well all season," she adds.

"Skate Canada was all right, but it was a pared down version of *Orchid*, and it was not of the standard that I expected *Orchid* to go to. And certainly they did not have a good run with it at the Grand Prix Final, and they did not have a go with it at the Canadian Championships.

"So to send somebody to the Olympics with a program that they are not feeling confident that they can do under pressure, would have been a very big mistake."

In the golden pair debate, Paul Wylie is on the fence with Miller.

"That night, I was so overwhelmed by how I felt the Canadians skated; they skated beautifully, but looking at the Russians, they also have an incredible quality to them. I do think Jamie and David had a slight edge, but for me it was almost a tie," he offers.

"And you could argue that it was. The alternate judge did vote for the Canadians, so at the end of the day it really was a tie: five votes for each team," he reasons.

Ironically, the one person who firmly believes the judges got it right the first time by giving Elena and Anton gold was Katia Gordeeva, the one-time chief nemesis (alongside late husband and partner Sergei Grinkov) of coach Moskvina and several of her previous teams.

"I thought Elena and Anton skated great. You must look at the whole quality of their skating—all of it together—that was a 6.0," she claims.

The media hoopla around the pair outcome was nothing short of a circus.

"A lot of emphasis was put on the judging, and while I know a lot of the scrutiny was justified, I felt it was like someone just yelled, 'Fire!' and everyone started running," explains Miller. "I don't think that's fair to the public. It would have been nicer for the sport and the public to have things explained. So at least the public can make a more educated opinion about things."

Asserts noted singles and pair coach John Nicks, "Yes, I thought the pairs result was in question, but the media exposure was biased. What worried me was the continual showing of Anton's one mistake. It was seen over and over again. It tended to overemphasize that aspect and not show many of the wonderful things the Russians did."

Undoubtedly, having the Winter Olympics in the U.S. and the "injured" party being North American added considerable fuel to the fire. "The media took hold of the controversy, and it became the thing to highlight. That was the story, and they ran with it. I don't think it would have happened in Europe or Japan," states Christopher Dean.

"They could have kept the story on the news, but I don't think it really needed to be on the cover of *Time* and *Newsweek*—the whole nine yards," contends Salt Lake pair competitor and three-time U.S. Champion John Zimmerman, who finished fifth with partner Kyoko Ina. "It was too much and spread like wildfire."

Adds former Olympic silver medalist Rosalynn Sumners, "It was a big deal, but on the front page of *USA Today*? Give me a break! For Dan Rather to start the *CBS Evening News*, 'Well, before we get to the war, a judging controversy.' It was a joke."

The two pair teams were caught up in the giant media wave and had little choice but to ride it out. Jamie and David, in particular, were put on the spot.

"The media started it all by putting Jamie and David in an impossible situation and begging them to give comments, so they did," offers Moskvina.

"Yet for two years in a row we accepted with dignity the results at the competitions in Canada, when all the judges were very kind to the Canadian skaters. We were silent. We never said, 'Oh, this is Canada. They are judging us wrong.'"

Moskvina's natural bias notwithstanding, there is remarkable sentiment in skating circles that Jamie and David—regardless of whether they should have won the event in the first place—broke an unwritten rule in figure skating by not just accepting the results.

"I was surprised that the Canadians brought it up afterwards. In an event, you skate and the judges decide. That's the way it is," states Gordeeva. "When I skated, no one talked after the competition about the results. It was over. I do understand that the Canadians did it because they thought they skated better, but I don't agree with it."

"I love Jamie and David. They're great kids. But it's like when you watch a football game, and in the last 10 seconds a player catches the ball in the end zone for a touchdown. Then you look at the replay and see that his foot was out of bounds, but it already counted. The game is over," says Zimmerman. "You're not going to bring back 50,000 people into the arena and replay the last 10 seconds just because it wasn't correct and the referee made a mistake. It's finished. You deal with it and go on."

Ilia Kulik, 1998 Olympic Men's gold medalist, agrees. "The athletes are there to compete and to accept the result," he says. "That's why there are judges. It makes your life a little bit easier, and you don't have to think about it. You do your job and accept what happens.

"If somebody doesn't believe the judges, then there is nobody to believe. I will be saying that I'm better, and he will be saying he is better, and so on. That's why the judges are there. It's best for skaters to stay focused on the skating, accept the results, move forward and improve."

Alexei Yagudin feels the Canadians' comments turned into whines and got out of hand. "After a while I was tired of listening to it. Sure, Jamie and David really won, but Elena and Anton were given the gold medal. You can't just say, 'Can we get a gold medal like Russia?' This is not fair. I've lost by unfair judging, but I've also won by unfair judging. Everyone has," he says.

On the other side, Paul Wylie and Philippe Candeloro applaud Jamie and David's actions. "It put accountability back in the hands of the stakeholders like the Canadian Olympic Association, the skaters and even the spectators. Usually, accountability takes place from the standpoint of the ISU Technical Committee, and that's the only place that accountabilities are exercised," explains Wylie.

"In this case, it was more realistic of the stakeholders of the sport. That's what I appreciated about the Olympics—there is so much attention on the sport that you wind up with a more realistic situation."

Frenchman Candeloro concurs. "Things happened and changed this time only because it was the Olympics and the Canadians were willing to open their mouths and say something, which they did because their federation supported them," he notes. "It's great.

"In the past I tried to do something similar, but my federation (Federation Française des Sports de Glace) didn't stand behind me, and nobody cares about the French federation anyway. It's a different story with Americans or Canadians."

Orser believes without the North American factor the second gold medal never would have happened.

"Jamie and David were extremely fortunate that the Olympics were here," he declares. "Anywhere else, forget it! There wouldn't have been the squawk, and it would have been forgotten after a couple of days. Instead, talk show hosts Jay Leno and Rosie O'Donnell were saying on their programs, 'What's wrong with this picture,' and stirring the pot more and more.

"Something had to be done right away, and the IOC panicked. And they panicked because their sponsors were disappointed. These are the people ultimately paying their salaries—millions and millions of dollars. These sponsors are questioning the integrity of the IOC, so something had to be done."

Adds Gordeeva, "It seems funny to award two gold medals and there be more than one champion. But in the end, nothing else could happen. In order to settle things, it was the best thing for both the Russians and the Canadians."

"The media buzz and frenzy got so out of control that awarding another gold medal became the only option. If they didn't, the integrity of skating really would have been jeopardized. In that sense I agree with it, but I was also shocked it happened," says Miller. "I don't think it will happen again or should happen again. It should have been explained better and handled better right off the top. Instead, everyone got so angry so fast."

Wylie and Nicks wonder how time will look back upon the snap decision to have two Olympic champions.

"There was a good reason for them to have the resolution of double gold, but sometimes real justice takes time. An immediate decision at the Olympics is satisfying, but I am not sure it was correct. It may have been a little rash when history looks at it," predicts Wylie.

"It's pretty obvious that it was rushed into as a result of encouragement from the IOC. Hopefully, the decision won't come back to haunt anyone. Hopefully, it won't provide an example," says Nicks.

That's the fear: that the door has now been opened for future, and even past, complaints.

"I completely disagree with giving a second gold medal, for that reason. Everybody in our sport who doesn't think that they got justly what they deserve is going to cry foul or file a protest," worries Lloyd Eisler.

"The Lithuanian dancers came up with a protest at the Olympics and Worlds demanding medals. It's ridiculous. But what happened at the Olympics with the pairs is the cause," concludes Bechke. "The whole craziness about the second gold medal set such a bad example. They shouldn't have done it. What's done is done. It shouldn't be undone, shouldn't even try to be."

"In my book, it was black and white that Jamie and David won, but I wasn't for the dual gold medals at all. Once you start giving them out, you are opening up Pandora's box. Everybody will be coming forward and saying they should have one," states 1988 Olympic silver medalist Liz Manley.

"The question people kept asking me at the Olympics was, now are you going to fight for your gold medal? The thing is, when you start giving out second gold medals, there are so many skaters who have lost five-to-four decisions at the Olympics, including myself, who could start complaining, 'Why didn't I get one?' So I would have left the medals alone."

Tai Babilonia says it opened up yet another can of worms, one the media never really concerned itself with. "Once they did the second gold, people wondered, shouldn't the third and fourth places and so on move up? That gets a little confusing, especially to the public. I had people come up to me and say 'So they did this, now what happens to the pairs in back of them? Do they automatically jump up a notch?'" she says.

That was exactly the thought of Kyoko Ina & John Zimmerman, who finished fifth in the Salt Lake pairs event, due to a five-to-four decision. Le Gougne had voted for the Russian team of Tatiana Totmianina & Maxim Marinin, instead of the U.S. team.

"Right after the decision was made to give Jamie and David a gold medal, Kyoko and I went on TV and were saying, if first and second place needed to be changed around or altered, then how does that affect the rest of the field?" recalls Zimmerman.

"We started to pursue it, since fourth and fifth place was decided by one swing vote (Le Gougne's). But then we decided not to, because we thought, if we're going to do this over fourth and fifth place—which absolutely means nothing, especially in the eyes of everyone else—we're going to look like a bunch of crybabies.

"I was surprised that no one picked on it. But the way the media operates is that they glorify one or two people, and no one else exists. They were done with it. It's not a super long-term type of story anyway. It's hot news real fast, then goes away."

Sharing a gold medal put them in the headlines, but it's not exactly something Elena and Anton and Jamie and David had envisioned for their Olympic dreams.

"It hurt both couples. Honestly, neither could be truly satisfied with the final result," offers Moskvina.

"But we refuse to dwell on it. We accepted with dignity the not-so-very-nice decision of the IOC to give two gold medals. Elena and Anton got the gold medal as we had planned. The rest doesn't matter."

For her part, Elena is happy, though, that she and Anton "had our medals first and received them after the competition."

David can understand. He admits getting the gold at the second medal ceremony was a little anticlimactic. "The moment itself was gone, along with the feeling you have right after your performance. Still it was a happy moment, but that unforgettable type of reaction was killed. So from that standpoint, it was definitely weird," he says.

Neither of the teams says they were asked for input on the unusual ceremony. "We were basically just told to show up. Obviously, if they had asked me how I would have liked to have had it, it would have been a little different. But hey, that's OK," says David.

"Honestly, it wasn't the way we wanted to have it, but you can't always have what you want. In the end, we were just so excited to get the gold medals," expresses Jamie.

"We were also really glad that the Russians came to the ceremony. They were good sports about it. It was hard on everybody. For them to come and show their support and share in it was wonderful."

Reflects David, "The best picture I've seen from that ceremony was a shot from the back of the podium, and there [are] Anton and I, and you see Russia and Canada on our jackets. And his flag is on my side and my flag is on his side. I thought that really summed everything up. It was the coolest picture."

"Everyone seems to forget that at the Olympics it was nothing against Elena and Anton. It was not even something to do with Jamie and myself. It had to do with the judging and the collusion," David states.

David and Jamie are very conscious that the controversy and second medal ceremony weren't easy situations for the Russians.

"I can't imagine being in Elena and Anton's shoes, where you have the gold medal, then you find out the judges were cheating. Then, all of a sudden, you shouldn't have won. You work your whole life to get there, and then after you're awarded the Olympic gold medal, you find they want to take it back in a way," says Jamie.

It wasn't an easy position, confirms Elena. "I was in shock when they started talking about two gold medals," she says. "I never thought such a thing would happen to me. But it did, and you make the best of it. You put it behind you and go on."

Both teams already had the experience in Salt Lake of putting unpleasant incidents behind them, after the free skating warm up in which Anton and Jamie had a major collision. And who's to say how that affected either skater's performance, for better or for worse?

"To be honest, I was frightened," admits Jamie. "Obviously, it was a total freak accident. Both of us were really shaken up. I could tell that Anton felt really bad, and I felt bad for him, too. I got the wind knocked out of me and couldn't breathe. That's what scared me the most when I got off the ice. If I had had to skate first, I don't know if I would have been able to. I simply couldn't breathe.

"I remember, I just took one look at Dave and thought, *Jamie, you've got to get yourself together. You don't have time to sit here and feel bad. You can't allow yourself to be in pain right now.* It's amazing what adrenaline does. It takes over. My pain just went away when I looked at Dave, and I thought, *I'm not giving up. This is my night. These people are pumped up. I'm pumped up. I'm ready and have worked my whole life for this.* That's how I got through.

"The next day I was a little sore, but two days after that, my ribs and my neck hurt. I got whiplash. I also got hit in the thigh. I was sore almost everywhere. I felt beaten up," she describes.

"If that had been in practice, I probably wouldn't have been able to skate anymore, but because it was in warm-up, I had so much adrenaline and got through it—without making a mistake. It was quite amazing."

Their entire Olympic odyssey was a real life lesson, says David.

"It was a great test as far as life goes, because all along we did say that we were going there to do our best, no matter the outcome. That's the way it's going to be, and we're going to be fine with it. Sometimes in life it's time to walk the talk. We did. We said all along that we came second, that's the way it was. But nobody likes to be cheated out of it. You want the chance to win," David explains.

"We learned, though, that no matter what you do in life, you do it for yourself," he continues. "That's where you get the real joy. You get something back from your work, from your effort, from your sweat and tears. You do it for yourself. You don't do it to win the gold, because you can't always control what goes on in life. Always focus on what you can control, not what you can't."

The French judge and federation president associated with all the pair drama received their comeuppance two months after Salt Lake.

In April, Marie-Reine Le Gougne and Didier Gailhaguet each received three-year suspensions from the ISU, effective immediately, and were also barred from participating at the 2006 Winter Games in Turin, Italy.

Both vowed to appeal. But as the date for the appeal approached, Gailhaguet chose not to file it, saying he was looking to re-establish relations with the ISU. Although she initially filed an appeal, Le Gougne subsequently announced she had decided to drop her action and instead will write a book.

Philippe Candeloro argues that Le Gougne and Gailhaguet benefited from their devious deeds and got exactly what they wanted.

"[Le Gougne] has always liked to be in the spotlight first. She always did things like all judges do, but she was the one who opened her mouth to say what she did or to show, 'Oh, I am here, and I did this, and I did this.' It was all to make her seem more important," asserts Candeloro.

"Now, she is like the biggest, most famous judge in the world, and Didier thinks he is the biggest man in the world. That counts with the French [skating] federation (Federation Française des Sports de Glace), so I think they have accomplished something."

This story, however, didn't end with the ISU's punishment of Le Gougne and Gailhaguet—far from it. To a certain extent, it had yet to scratch the surface.

On July 31, the FBI arrested Alimzhan Tokhtakhounov, identified by the FBI as a member of Russian organized crime, and charged him with influencing members of the Russian and French skating federations to rig the outcomes of the pair and ice dancing competitions at the 2002 Olympics.

He allegedly masterminded the scheme to win favor with influential French sports officials (including Gailhaguet), in an attempt to obtain a renewal of his French visa, as he hoped to reside in that country again. According to the FBI, Tokhtakhounov's rap sheet includes drug distribution, trafficking in stolen vehicles, illegal gun sales and the fixing of Moscow beauty pageants.

The federal case against him is based primarily on bugged telephone conversations recorded earlier this year, courtesy of authorities in Italy, the country in which he now spends most of his time. Those wiretaps caught Tokhtakhounov speaking with several unidentified co-conspirators.

One is allegedly a member of the Russian figure skating federation, with whom Tokhtakhounov discussed the plot to fix the two Olympic events.

And though not addressed by name, the common thought is that 2002 Olympic Ice Dance Champion Marina Anissina is the French ice dancer on tape. The taped ice dancer's mother spoke to Tokhtakhounov as well.

The Russian-born and -raised Anissina moved to France in 1993 to skate with partner Gwendal Peizerat.

Tokhtakhounov refers to Anissina as "one of ours" to the Russian skating official, who replied, "Thank you, she will be grateful to you for the rest of her life."

Prior to Tokhtakhounov's arrest, Gwendal Peizerat spoke about how unlikely it was that the pair controversy affected the dance results.

"I felt this was something that happened in pairs, not in ice dance—so for one time we may have a fair ice dance competition, because they wanted to take care to ensure that it went properly," he noted. "This whole thing will scare them from doing some crazy stuff. Everyone will watch what they are doing. What happened in pairs had no impact on me."

Nearly a week after the FBI bombshell hit the public, Anissina finally admitted she knows Tokhtakhounov, but staunchly denies being involved in any conspiracy or knowledge of one.

"Gwendal and myself didn't need anyone to win our gold medal at Salt Lake City. The experts are unanimous regarding this, and neither the taped boasts of certain people nor manipulation attempts by others will change anything," asserts Anissina. "The mark of the Russian judge at the Olympics against us speaks for itself!"

True, the Russian judge in ice dance voted for the Russian team, eventual Olympic silver medalists Irina Lobacheva & Ilia Averbukh, instead of Anissina and Peizerat. This point is what the Russians hang their hat on as the "proof" that no quid-pro-quo deal for pairs and dance was in place.

But the reality is that the reach of the Russian figure skating system is far and wide. Russian-born judges generally make up the panels for Belarus, Ukraine and other republics that were once all included under the Soviet Union. Coincidentally, Yuki Balkov, the Ukrainian judge in the Olympic ice dance event, did vote for the French. And Balkov is no stranger to voting controversies.

He was caught on tape by Canadian judge Jean Senft as he tried to fix the results of the 1998 Olympic ice dance competition. Balkov outlined the final results before the event took place. He was suspended by the ISU for one season, then resumed judging.

When asked why the ISU's two-month inquiry into the pair scandal, which led to the suspensions of Le Gougne and Gailhaguet, did not include investigating the Russians, ISU President Ottavio Cinquanta replied, "We cannot work on fantasy or unfounded allegations. We need evidence and we had none. We cannot accuse on the basis of point of view."[1]

Former ISU Technical Committee Chairperson Sally Stapleford completely disagrees. She had been the one Le Gougne confessed to in the hotel lobby, and she reported the encounter to Cinquanta in writing.

"She (Le Gougne) said she had not judged correctly. That the president of the French skating federation (FFSG) and ISU Council member Didier Gailhaguet had put her under pressure to have the Russian pair first over the Canadians, and that it was a deal with the Russians in connection with the ice dance event. She stated over and over again how ice dancing was causing so much trouble," proclaims Stapleford.

Stapleford says she now feels vindicated. She had pushed to investigate the Russians all along. In June, she failed in her bid for re-election as chairwoman of the ISU Figure Skating Technical Committee, losing to Alexander Lakernik, of Russia, who just happened to be the assistant referee for the Olympic pair event.

The ISU's behavior and the current crisis at its door do not amuse the IOC.

"I would be real worried if I were figure skating," cautions IOC member Dick Pound, of Canada. "If your results make a complete mockery of what happens on the ice, people aren't going to put kids into skating, and that will cause it to dry up."[2]

Pound, who for years has referred to ice dancing as the root of skating's problems, thinks now is the time to finally pull the plug on it until reforms are made.

IOC Vice President Thomas Bach suggests that voiding the Salt Lake City figure skating outcomes is not out of the question. "I am not ruling out anything, not even the annulment of the Olympic results."[3]

The skaters obviously under the most scrutiny are Anissina and Peizerat, since the dance outcome was the scheme's goal. They say they aren't concerned about it and have no reason to be.

Likewise, Moskvina is not worried about the IOC looking into Elena and Anton.

"If the FBI needs to, let them investigate the deals surrounding the medals, let them do that. We didn't do anything wrong. We never had any connections with anybody in the Russian Mafia.

"They can check our bank accounts. We didn't have any transactions. We needed money, and that's why we came to the United States: so Elena and Anton could participate in shows and earn money. If we had connections with the Mafia, we never would have come. We would have stayed home and have that money from the Mafia and live very nicely."

"If the athletes did not know anything about the wrongdoing, I feel sorry for them because they are victims of the situation that maybe they were not aware of," says Victor Kraatz, who, along with partner Shae-Lynn Bourne, finished just out of the ice dance medals in Salt Lake City.

While Kraatz obviously has a vested interest in any medals changing hands, he knows that any real talk of that is premature. "We have to wait until everything, all the angles, have been looked at and see if all these allegations are true. With the FBI involved, there is going to be a thorough investigation. And whatever happens, happens."

So the skating world waits.

Like Anissina and Gailhaguet, Tokhtakhounov claims innocence. Was he the mastermind behind the entire Salt Lake judging controversy or simply a big time braggart?

The FBI investigation likely has months to go. Whether there is a smoking gun that the IOC would need to strip medals remains to be seen.

After a series of meetings in late August, the IOC did not appear to be taking any steps to change the ice dance results. At that time, Tokhtakhounov sat in a jail cell in Venice, Italy, while lawyers battled against his extradition to the U.S.

Though it pales in comparison to the continuing saga of Salt Lake, the bitterly disputed ice dance result at the 2002 World

Championships in Nagano, Japan, was a debacle in its own right.

Under attack were Israel's Galit Chait & Sergey Sakhnovsky. The ice dancers were accused of buying the bronze medal, courtesy of Galit's father Boris Chait.

"A skater came up to me right after the results come up and asked, 'How much did the medal cost?'" recounts Sakhnovsky.

"Nobody can probably fight with the big money which is involved in the moving up of the Israeli couple. How else can you explain the result?" questions Povilas Vanagas, who finished fourth alongside partner and wife Margarita Drobiazko.

Galit Chait's father, Boris Chait, categorically denies giving money to any judges or officials. And despite all of the talk of his bribery, no one has yet come forward offering any evidence.

"I just don't understand. We gave it all we had in the compulsory dances, the original dance and the free dance. We skated the free dance full out, 100 percent. We gave it all we had. No mistakes," contends Galit Chait.

After the awards ceremony, Chait and Sakhnovsky suffered quite a shock when they arrived back to the athletes' hotel. Nearly all of their competitors in the free dance, 38 in total, were signing a petition that read:

> **On behalf of all of the undersigned skaters in the ice dance event, we would like to bring to your attention our discontent with the final results of the competition. We are particularly distressed with the awarding of the bronze medal. In our opinion, the Lithuanians (Drobiazko and Vanagas) skated a medal worthy performance, and were not awarded for their outstanding performance. For the sake and integrity of our sport, we would like some kind of clarification as to how this could happen. It seemed clear to all of those watching the event that the third place was not justified and fairly awarded.**

Additionally, there was a separate petition signed by several coaches and one judge.

"I was surprised that the dancers organized together, but you know, I would have signed that petition if I had been there," says three-time U.S. Ice Dance Champion Renée Roca.

"I felt like the skaters were trying to make a statement and have their own voice and express what they really felt, because it is their event. They are the ones actually in it, skating it and involved. Why shouldn't they express what they really, really feel and make a stand, a statement? Good for them!"

Not surprisingly, Galit Chait didn't see it that way. "They took the sweetest moment that we had and destroyed it for us," she states.

That consequence was of little concern to the other ice dancers, who felt a stand needed to be taken for the sake of their sport.

"It's the first time athletes are actually speaking out about the judging. Hopefully, everyone will realize that the athletes are fed up," says U.S. Ice Dance Champion Naomi Lang, who finished ninth in the event with partner Peter Tchernyshev.

"When the athletes come together in such a unified opinion and they're willing to put their names on the line, that should be a very loud and clear call to the ISU that there is a significant problem," declares U.S. judge Sharon Rogers, who says she received anonymous death threats following the free dance at Worlds.

Upon witnessing his emotionally distraught daughter, Boris Chait went to a room at the athletes' hotel where some of the coaches were having a party. He angrily confronted Alexander Zhulin, then-coach of Lang and Tchernyshev and still the coach of Russian ice dancers Tatiana Navka (Zhulin's wife) & Roman Kostomarov.

"If they want to express their opinions, let them express it," insists Boris Chait. "Why they do it, who instigated it and how it was done is a different story."

The petition went forward and was presented the following day to the ISU Ice Dance Technical Committee, which was holding its annual meeting with skaters and coaches.

"It was worth noting that the skaters' petition occurred," says Ann Shaw, a member of the Ice Dance Technical Committee. "The skaters have an opinion. I don't know how you measure the validity in terms of having actually sat there and judged the event."

At a separate review meeting of the World Championships, Courtney Jones, ice dance event referee and member of the Ice Dance Technical Committee, refused to allow the judges to discuss the results of third and fourth place and threatened sanctions on anyone who spoke about the meeting publicly.

The ISU denied the petition, and the results remained the same. Subsequently, the Lithuanian Skating Federation filed an additional protest with the ISU, but that also went nowhere.

Ice dance legend Christopher Dean ponders, "Maybe the dancers will eventually have to form their own union, because there is no real representation for the skaters within the ISU. Something has to be done."

Indeed, the skaters tried that in 1995. They held a meeting at the World Championships in Birmingham, England, and formed the International Figure Skaters Association. But a proposed meeting at the 1996 World Championships never materialized, and, ultimately, everyone forgot about it. Although it may meet with renewed enthusiasm, to date no one has made a move to reintroduce it.

The lasting effect these two controversies will have on the sport remains to be seen. Will figure skating really clean up its act?

A story of Babilonia's from Salt Lake City should serve as great motivation.

"I was at the pairs final, and afterwards, I went to the bathroom. After I came out of the stall, a woman who obviously recognized me came running up. She was waving her ticket stub in my face and said, 'I paid $275 to be lied to!' She was so upset about the result. All I could say was, 'I'm sorry, and I understand your feeling. I don't get the result either.'

"She was so pissed that she paid so much money and didn't get a fair result. I didn't blame her at all. It's reactions like hers that should worry the ISU and skating, because people, the audience, are really how skating makes its money."

Things have to change, insists Zimmerman, who was glad to see his sport's dirty little secret exposed.

"It makes me sick that nine people that you don't even know come in and have other plans for you, no matter what you do, how you skated—instead of judging with their own conscience," he says.

"We skaters have spent thousands of hours, thousands of dollars, in our lifetime for the opportunity to compete for a reputable Winter Games. And here nine people screw it all up for us. It's really irritating. It has to be remedied."

[1] Vicki Michaelis, *USA Today*, July 31, 2002

[2] Mike Todd, *USA Today*, August 1, 2002

[3] Associated Press, August 2, 2002

The Verdict Is In

13

"Anytime you have a sport that is subjective,
it's difficult, because it's basically somebody's
opinion as to whether you are good or not."

– Michael Weiss,
two-time U.S. Men's Champion,
two-time World bronze medalist

The Verdict
Is In

S katers give their entire lives and all their energies to be a part of something special. They should be honored with a good system of judging—one where everybody who takes part in the sport or watches it feels comfortable about the result," says 1984 Olympic Men's Champion Scott Hamilton, who served as a television commentator at the last four Olympic Winter Games. "The sport has been so compromised by the events in Salt Lake City that we need that more than ever."

As the 2002 Olympic pair controversy lingers like a black cloud, the great debate concerns exactly what should be done about the judging.

People in the skating community are at both ends of the spectrum—and everywhere in between.

Many feel a change in the actual judging system is necessary to restore the sport's credibility and tarnished reputation.

Some current and former skaters strongly disagree. They argue nothing was wrong with the method by which skaters were judged. Instead, the problem comes down to a few corrupt judges who are ruining it for everybody; go deal with those people, and find a way to ensure it doesn't happen again. Still others believe focusing on the judging at all is a lost cause.

Meanwhile, ISU President Ottavio Cinquanta contends that radical reconstructive surgery is, in the end, the only remedy.

Cinquanta wants to eliminate the 6.0 measuring stick skaters have always known. It will be replaced with a cumulative points system, one that potentially rewards athleticism over artistry. Additionally, the size of the judging panel is to be altered, increasing to 14 members, with nine selected randomly and anonymously to determine the result.

The notion of abolishing the 6.0 standard has set the figure skating world on its ear.

Some fear that in pursuit of obtaining as many points as possible, creativity and grace—the very things that make skating so unique—will be lost.

In June, the ISU Congress met in Kyoto, Japan, to decide the course of action.

A complete overhaul of the system like Cinquanta advocates cannot happen quickly. It will take a skating season or two to test and then implement. Wanting to show action now, the Congress adopted a proposal by the Canadian federation, Skate Canada, which, coincidentally, is in line with Cinquanta's ultimate intent.

Twenty judges will be in attendance at ISU events and 14 will be randomly selected to judge. Only nine judges' scores, chosen randomly and anonymously by computer, will determine the outcome. For now, the 6.0 system remains in place.

The increased judging panel debuts at ISU Championships—World Junior Championships, European Championships, Four Continents Championships and the World Championships—this 2002–03 season. Events in the Grand Prix—such as Skate America, Skate Canada and Cup of Russia—remain unaffected, although tests of the new system will be run at some of the competitions.

Reactions to the immediate change are mixed.

"It's tough to say if it will make a difference," offers pair skater David Pelletier, whose Skategate experiences in Salt Lake City are part of the initiative for change. "You know, it's not all the judges who don't judge fairly. There are just a few rotten apples, and if they are still there under the new system, I don't know how good it's going to get."

Fellow Canadian Brian Orser is excited, though. "I'm really intrigued to have the 14-member judging panel and to randomly select which marks are going to count. It's virtually impossible to make a deal. The deal goes up in smoke if the marks of the country you made a deal with don't count, and you won't know that until the end."

Brian Boitano isn't so convinced the new twist to the system is foolproof. "What's going to keep them from trading votes again? What's going to keep them from making deals with several people and countries?"

Current Olympic and World Men's Champion Alexei Yagudin doesn't like the random selection aspect at all, believing it could provide outcomes that wouldn't happen under the old system. "The first nine judges can put me in first and the last five judges have me in second. And the computer chooses to include the last five. It's ridiculous."

Paul Wylie is concerned with the secrecy of the selections. "I'm not in support of it. There is no transparency. While the event is happening, you don't know who the judges are and the way they are judging," he says.

A few skaters are hung up on the fact that the revised system doesn't solve the subjectivity factor, aka the presentation or artistic impression mark, which may or may not continue to be scored based on 6.0. Others believe opinion is just a part of skating's fabric and must be accepted as such.

"The artistic mark is what really screws up a lot of it," declares 1988 Olympic Women's silver medalist Liz Manley. "An artistic mark is a mark for a judge to do whatever he/she wants with a skater—whether they like them or not."

Two-time U.S. Men's Champion Michael Weiss holds a more understanding view. "My opinion is obviously completely different than somebody born and raised in Russia," he says. "And that's normal."

Adds former U.S. Pair Champion Jenni Meno, "When you're judging, you're supposed to be following rules, but there's a lot of personal opinion involved, especially on the second mark. It's bound to happen in anything that's judged like this.

"The thing is that as a high-level competitive figure skater, you can't control what happens with the judging. You try to go out and put out your best skating and let the chips fall where they may."

Since there will always be a certain level of bias and subjectivity in skating, what's the point of eventually abandoning the 6.0 system?

Across the board, the skaters simply can't see one.

"There's nothing wrong with it. What's wrong is the fact that the Ukrainian and Russian judges are back judging a couple of years after their suspensions for cheating—and one was on the panel at the 2002 Olympics," declares Orser, referring to

256

Ukrainian ice dance judge Yuri Balkov, who was present on the ice dance panel in Salt Lake City, despite being suspended for judging improprieties committed at the 1998 Olympics. "That was the most ridiculous thing I've ever seen. The ISU brought these crooked judges right back and let them on the panels."

True, it is the ISU that brought them back. The ISU sets a time for the suspension, and once the suspension is served, the judges are eligible to judge again. The ISU also names the countries that are eligible to judge an event, and the nations name the judge of their choice. It is the Ukrainian Figure Skating Federation that put Balkov's name forth, and the ISU had no choice but to allow him to judge. A proposal to put all championship judges (judges qualified to judge at Worlds and Olympics) under the banner of the ISU (instead of national federations) was defeated at the ISU Congress in 2000.

But Cinquanta is determined to implement his cumulative scoring system, and the ISU is currently working on it for "completion as soon as possible." At the 2002 Congress in Kyoto, Cinquanta's system was accepted as a "project" to be tested over the next two years.

"Ottavio's system will totally change the way of judging. The basis is completely different," says USFSA President Phyllis Howard, newly elected member of the ISU Council.

Under the current system, skaters receive marks that reflect deductions made from a 6.0 scoring cap. These deductions are based on a set of variables, including completion or omission of an element and its quality. After reviewing the content in a program, the judge sets a base mark—either at 6.0 or below—from which they take the deductions.

Skaters receive two separate marks—technical merit and presentation—which are what the audience sees. These scores are added together, and the skater who receives the highest point total from a judge receives that judge's number one placement or first place ordinal. (In case of a tie in the total, the higher technical merit mark wins out in the technical or short program, and the higher presentation score decides the long or free program.)

For example, at the 2002 Olympics, Sarah Hughes beat Irina Slutskaya for the gold by a five-to-four split of the ordinals in the long program. Sarah had five first places from the judges to Irina's four first places.

At those Olympics, Hughes was trailing Michelle Kwan (whom she beat in the free skate) until after Slutskaya skated. That is known as switching—where positions change places due to the performance of another skater. The ISU computation system, called OBO, slightly modifies the basic computation. This system was implemented in 1999 to cause less place-switching—something that Cinquanta has always found objectionable, because members of the media who are not well educated on the sport of figure skating often complain about it. Under OBO (an acronym for One By One), each skater's scores are compared against every other skater's scores, and a total is made for the number of times the skater tops the other skaters. The USFSA has never adopted this system for U.S. Nationals.

Under Cinquanta's new plan, the individual scores of the judges are not translated into ordinals or placements, but remain as numbers and are added together to produce a final total that determines the winner. This final mark is what the audience sees.

On top of that, each element of a skater's program will be assigned a score according to an agreed scale of difficulty, plus or minus a score for the quality of execution (such as poor, mediocre, good or excellent). Scores for all technical elements and their grades of execution, plus the scores for general skating skills (i.e., speed, stroking and carriage) will be added to a presentation score, which is probably still scored on a 6.0. This sum represents a judge's final mark for each skater.

For instance, a double axel jump could be worth three points, a combination spin, two points, and a triple lutz, five points. Subjectivity comes into play when determining the quality of the completed element.

"I may think something was excellent, you may think it was poor. We both can agree they landed the jump. Still, there is room for a big divergence of opinion," states Howard. "Maybe I like a quad jump that goes up higher, but doesn't travel as far across the ice."

Another kicker is that the skater who would win under the ordinal system may not be the winner under the cumulative system.

Each judge's score is critical under the cumulative system and counts toward the final placement. Under the ordinal system, if you garner five judges—a majority of the panel—it doesn't matter if the other four judges have you second, third, fifth and tenth. That only factors in if no skater has a majority of first places.

"The two systems are like apples and oranges, because if you compare the results and the results are different, does it mean that the different results are wrong? It means they are always comparing against the ordinal system," assesses Howard.

And for a media corps that has battled to understand and communicate details about ordinals, OBO and factored placements, won't this be even more difficult to explain?

Wylie says the system is trying to set a high standard for the ultimate performance, yet one is already in place. "There is a standard, and there will always be a standard. The perfect mark should be what the highest standard is at that time. For men now, it should be two quads and seven triples or whatever," he says. "And you shouldn't be able to get a 6.0 in technical merit unless you are doing all of that to perfection. To me, that's pretty clear. I don't think we need to change it, just follow that guide."

Wylie is also concerned with the reality of the additive marking aspect of the cumulative system. "It's not a good idea. You start to really obscure what the program is, what the technical elements are, and you also cause the judges to have to go through a tremendous mathematical exercise," he states.

Indeed. Judges will have to keep track of where the selected element is on the agreed scale of difficulty, note that and then assign a quality of execution mark to it. This will be done for every element. So instead of punching in a 5.8 at the conclusion of a program, judges appear to have to issue marks as they go or do it in a flurry at the end.

"Unless they have some sort of voice recognition software where they can speak into something, they will be looking down every second somebody does something, either to write down the element and grade or making a selection off a computer screen or Palm Pilot," Wylie says.

"In the end, the judges and the audience at home are sitting there thinking, 'That performance was a 5.9.' They are not sitting there going, 'That was a 355.4.' We can't afford to make our sport more esoteric to the public. It must be understandable, and it must be distillable."

Sally Stapleford, chairwoman of the ISU Figure Skating Technical Committee from 1992–2002, agrees that such a radical change should be carefully scrutinized. "One should consider looking at all ideas to improve the judging system, but also we should retain what is good in the current system, and not 'throw the baby out with the bath water,'" she says.

Alexander Lakernik, the new chair of the ISU Figure Skating Technical Committee states, "You must always be able to keep your head clear during competition. Another thing is the ability to make decisions. There are some people who can't judge very well, because they are not capable of making decisions."

The new system with its many variables makes the process that much more stressful and complicated for a corps of judges that is already dwindling.

Many in skating circles feel that neither what has been implemented for this season nor Cinquanta's ultimate version will fix the real issue: corruption among judges and federations.

"If they try to fix the judging by going around that problem instead of attacking it head on, it's like fixing a broken arm with Novocain. What good is that?" quips Scott Hamilton.

So what really needs to happen with judging?

1. Accountability

"For starters, there needs to be some," declares Wylie. "Right now, judges can do whatever they want, and federations can get away with whatever they want. There needs to be some real sanctions, dismissals and, if something is proven, then kind of a 'three strikes and you're out' rule."

Stapleford suggests taking things a step further and "banning for life judges found guilty of misconduct."

The USFSA made just such a proposal at the ISU Congress, but it was not accepted.

In years past, the ISU Technical Committees had greater latitude to issue judge suspensions, but amendments at the Congress in 1998 shifted some of that power to the ISU Council—thus making it that much more difficult to administer swift action.

The old approach may be what cut short the judging career of David Dore, the leader of figure skating in Canada from 1985 to

January 2002. He was suspended from judging by the ISU for one year in 1984, based on the national bias he showed toward the top Canadian pair team Barbara Underhill & Paul Martini at the 1984 Olympics and to Canadian teams at the preceding Skate America competition. This information never became general public knowledge, because Dore simply never returned to judging. Instead, he accepted the paid position as director of the Canadian Figure Skating Association.

In 2002, after resigning as Director General of Skate Canada (the new name the CFSA has adopted), Dore applied for reinstatement of his eligible status. In June, he was elected vice president of the ISU. He is now one of the individuals responsible for determining judge sanctions and suspensions.

Michael Weiss would like to see accountability and punishment focused squarely on the federations. "Right now, if a judge does something improper, that judge may be suspended, but then the country just goes ahead and sends another judge," he says. "They put another one in there, and the same thing happens.

"There is no punishment or repercussion for the federation. But if you deprive that country of a judge if one was caught cheating, that would make a lot more sense. The countries and federations would then be less likely to cheat, if they feared not having a judge next year at Worlds if they were caught. Then the tables may turn, and federations will put pressure on their judges to not show bias or make deals."

Suspending an entire fleet of judges from a federation has actually happened before, says Benjamin Wright, member of the ISU Technical Committee from 1973–92 and its Chairperson from 1988–92.

"In 1978, all of the Soviet Union judges were suspended for two years," he recalls. It has been tried since, too. "In 1999, the ISU

Figure Skating Technical Committee proposed a sanction against French and Hungarian judges (figure skating only, not dance), having tracked them since 1996. The Committee recommended that they be suspended, but the ISU Council rejected it," shares Wright.

2. Separation

"Judges are still very much dependent on each individual country and their association. If the judges were to be hired by the skating body (ISU), then there would be less likelihood for bias, and they would have to go with what they see, as opposed to what they were told," assesses Canadian ice dancer Victor Kraatz.

"The judges get corrupted because the federations push them. The judges get approached by people all of the time. They are human beings and not always strong enough to resist. So the judges need to be completely independent of their federation," advises 1992 Olympic Pair silver medalist Elena Bechke, who is from Russia and now lives in the U.S.

"The judges should be like the jury in the U.S. court system and have no real contact with anyone. But it's so hard, because people are people and they want to talk. People should just be more honest."

Stapleford would like to see this separation take place at the earliest possible time in an official's career. "I would like to see judges/referees being taken completely out of the control of their respective members immediately after they are made international competition judges. The member would have no connection at all with the judges (therefore eliminating any pressure that certain members may put on their judges to judge in a certain way), with the ISU to nominate/select all the referees/judges for all the competitions and championships."

Hamilton contends, "Until you can separate those individuals from their host countries and allow them to judge on their own merit, there will always be a level of compromise, and it's really going to be hard for people to be comfortable with the results."

Just this scenario was proposed at the ISU Congress in 2000; however, it was not enacted. Supposedly, French judge Marie-Reine Le Gougne spoke about this failed proposal during her infamous outburst at the judges' review meeting for the pair event at the Olympics.

3. Compensation

"One of the things the ISU has done is create a big wedge between the skaters and the judges, because they have increased the amount of money the skaters are earning at competitions and have not done anything for the judges," states Kraatz.

"I would like to see the judges treated like real professionals," proposes Manley. "A lot of them are volunteers and doing this on their own time. If we started treating them like the Super Bowl referee, we would probably see change. They are paid good salaries and do their jobs respectfully and legally."

4. Proportionality

There is a way to equalize the power of the different regions of the skating world. "Have geographical zones for the draws of the panel of judges for all ISU Championships," suggests Stapleford.

Wylie concurs. "Perhaps there are four regions in the world, and there would be a proportion of judges picked for each event from each region," he says. "Then there would be a proportional representation of judges from different regions of the world, so no one region dominates.

"The breakup of the Soviet Union definitely causes greater weight to former Soviet republics that have been trained by that system. This would remedy the situation."

5. Education

"Improve the judges' education system, where possible, and start the education system in the countries where they have very little judges' education prior to becoming a judge for international competition. Also, have an examination before they become a judge of international competition," recommends Stapleford. At present, there are judges judging important events, such as the Grand Prix, who have never had an ISU exam. There is no exam until they apply to judge at the championship level—for Europeans and Worlds.

"Education is vital, and we need to use coaches and other experts in other fields that can help to produce well educated, knowledgeable, honest, confident judges and referees," she adds.

Barbara Fusar-Poli, the 2001 World Ice Dance Champion with Maurizio Margaglio, couldn't agree more.

"We had new rules this past year in dance, but the judges didn't always pay attention. They have to really understand them, follow them and see the competition—and judge what is happening, not what they want to see or what the politics want or what is happening in practice," she declares.

Boitano firmly believes judges need to have been skaters themselves.

"They have to have competed as skaters at a high level and have them tested by skaters, not officials, to make sure they know what they are seeing," he urges. "I know that in front of officials I could lay out a different entry into a triple lutz, and they would think it was a triple toe loop. And I couldn't pull that trick on any skaters."

Boitano went as far as to say he has always felt better being judged in the professional ranks as opposed to his amateur days, because the pro judges were skaters who "know what's BS and what's not."

"I can go up to them and say, 'How could you have given that technical mark to so-and-so. I did this and this.' Skaters just know. If you haven't skated, they use all this BS about, well, their spinning was a little bit better, and their footwork traveled more—all of this stuff is mumbo jumbo. Skaters don't listen to that. It's so important to have judges that competed at a high level themselves."

Concludes Hamilton, "Until every official who judges the World Championships or Olympic Games is an ISU official, is professional, compensated and there on their own merit—and can be removed for having a lack of merit—then you will not have a purely-judged event."

Others feel judging is a battle that can't be won or simply shouldn't be waged. Skating is skating. Accept if for what it is—warts and all—and go on.

"You could poll 10 people who have medaled at the Olympics in the past five Winter Games, and at some point in their careers, they have been shafted. That's not being negative. It's just the reality of our sport. We're asking nine people to subjectively judge us, and no nine people have the same opinion," says two-time Olympic Pair bronze medalist Lloyd Eisler.

"There were many times I honestly felt I was misjudged, and there's nothing you can do about it. Or there were other times where I felt other skaters were wronged. You make your choice to be in a judged sport," explains choreographer and former pair skater Lea Ann Miller. "It can make you angry, and you can use that anger in a positive way by working harder, or you can walk away and say, 'I don't want to be in a sport that's judged. I want to be in a sport where you cross the finish line.' It's your call."

Olympic Ice Dance gold medalist Gwendal Peizerat takes an interesting viewpoint. "I don't think the judges really did hold my fate in their hands," he says. "My opinion is that whenever we missed something in a competition, we gave them a little bit of something that would allow them to put us second or not give us what we deserved. Whenever you don't give them any room, then they can't do it. It's maybe not true, but it's how I feel and how I thought while I competed."

He also believes the judges are as much victims as the athletes in the skating world. "They are, as much as we skaters are, taken by the old system. It's not one person's fault or a group of persons' fault, like the judges. It's more a question of a system that has been built for years and has been in existence now for a long time," reasons Gwendal.

"So for me, to be bitter would be refusing the evolution of the sport and how it has been going on for years and years.

"I felt liberated a long time ago when I realized that the most important judgment of my skating was mine and the public's. When I felt that I skated good and had a good feeling on the ice, and when I feel like the public enjoyed it and I got a reward by my skaters, my buddies and coaches."

Offers Weiss, "A lot of times there is an unwritten protocol that goes on in figure skating—sort of a pecking order—and you just know that these things happen. It's happened to everybody, and skaters just accept aspects like this in our sport and have learned to deal with them."

Venerable coach John Nicks states, "I started skating competitively internationally in 1948 and continued for four to five years. Then I've been in this as a coach for 41 years, 33 as a U.S., World and Olympic coach. There have been problems with the judging from day one, from the very minute I stepped on the ice in St. Moritz at the 1948 Olympics. It's never stopped, and I don't think it ever will stop. Judging may be changed, but there will always be issues, complications and disagreements."

"Dishonesty in judging is no different than smuggling or cheating on your taxes ... eventually somebody gets caught," declares Eisler. "Does that mean it's going to stop? No. Will there be ramifications and changes made? Yes. Will that ultimately detour people from doing it in the future? No. Where there's a will, there's usually a way."

It's now in the hands of the ISU to develop a will for the future.

Kristi, Scott and a Cast of Thousands

14

"I look at skating now, and I see where it's headed. I think a real strong aspect of skating, and what makes it so great and so popular with the American public and the public around the world, is starting to diminish."

– *Scott Hamilton*

Kristi, Scott and a Cast of Thousands

A t the onset of the 21st century, figure skating finds itself facing a myriad of dilemmas.

Epic judging scandal. Dwindling pro scene. Legends in the twilight of their careers.

Where does all of this leave the sport?

Will a revival be around the corner?

Or is the worst yet to come?

Some of figure skating's greatest stars and business minds have no shortage of opinions.

"I've noticed that there hasn't been much of a frenzy after the Salt Lake Olympics, like we've seen in the past. You always counted on an Olympic year to be a great year to sell a lot of tickets, and this time it wasn't as noticeable," offers Brian Orser.

"I'm not sure why, because we certainly had some major stars and some great skating. The pairs judging controversy got a ton of media, but it didn't draw a lot of people back to the arenas to watch skating."

Noted agent and entrepreneur Michael Rosenberg echoes the sentiment.

"The Salt Lake Olympics were supposed to be the big bump that skating needed and what we had all anticipated for the past three years, but it didn't happen. The reason it didn't happen was because of the judging fiasco. Unfortunately, Salt Lake left a horrible taste in people's mouths regarding the sport itself—versus the Tonya/Nancy episode, which was a wonderful bump for the sport, because it centered on two personalities: the evil and the good," he explains. "The television ratings today are terrible, and attendance of the shows is disappointing."

Rosenberg predicts things will get even darker before they get brighter.

"I expect skating do be down further this year and the next year," states Rosenberg. "It will be very tough times for skating. In 2003 to 2005, it will hit rock bottom.

"Then, per history, it will start resurging again. New stars will emerge, and the popularity of the sport will start rising once more. The question becomes its base of popularity, and its base, unfortunately, is getting older. Skating needs to attract new, young fans to the sport."

That's a tough task, believes Brian Boitano.

"The interest of the American public is hard to keep. Nowadays, you've got to mix things up in what you're doing, because the audience gets bored," he says.

"That's one of the big problems with skating: there's really nothing fresh. Our sport is sort of reactionary to what's popular; it's never a pioneer. It doesn't go out on a limb, and it's not a visionary. That's what is important in this day and age. If something's popular, our sport will start to incorporate that—but by the time they do that, it's too late—instead of going out there and creating new things and different looks.

"Our sport has never been that way, and that's where it has to improve to really get the audience back that it wants and to create a different sort of look for young people to like the sport again."

Sports executive Mike Burg seconds that. "Skating is the furthest thing from hip," he says. "The people who watch it are mostly women over 55. That's the problem; it's not reaching the young set."

Others, like Ilia Kulik, feel figure skating simply goes in cycles and see no reason to panic over its current state.

"Skating was big, and it will be big. It has its own audience. Once people get in love with the sport, they stay with it. They never quit watching skating because of something like one judging incident. It will not stop people from loving the sport," he suggests.

"There are competitions, plus a bunch of great skaters you can sit and admire. The moving style in skating is so unique. It combines the speed with ballet shapes, the high jumps, incredible speed and choreography. It looks great. I don't think there is anything that can really take people away from it."

Furthermore, *Stars on Ice* choreographer and former U.S. Ice Dance Champion Michael Seibert contends that most people weren't so taken aback or put off by what happened in Salt Lake.

"Sure, the Olympic scandal did taint the system to some degree. But also, for as far back as I can remember, I don't think that the public didn't think that's part of skating. That's why a lot of people disregard skating in the first place, because they know it's judged, and when there is judging, there are conflicts of interest," says Seibert—who'd be one to know, having been pushed out of a bronze medal at the 1984 Olympics.

"I certainly don't think that anybody before these Olympics thought that skating was above reproach in terms of judging. The fact that it happened—while it may have a long-term impact—is the very nature of skating."

Out of all this mayhem needs to come a better definition of what skating is, says Rosalynn Sumners. "Are we a sport or entertainment? We are both, but when it goes to judging, which emphasis are you going to put the judging on?" she questions. "You have to fix the judging in the eligible competitions so it goes back to being judged as sport, as opposed to entertainment, with so much emphasis on the artistic side."

Beyond this, Sumners wonders what even would be the next step for skating. "That's the thing. I don't know where else that you can quite take skating. Where else can it possibly go from here? It can't get bigger than it was in the 90s. You're not going to get much bigger personalities than Scott Hamilton and Michelle Kwan."

"Figure skating is for sure not a growth sport anymore. But I don't think that means it can't grow," offers Bob Kain, President and COO, Americas, IMG. "But it's going to have its peaks and valleys and may have its Olympic cycles. Certain personalities will spike it a little bit, but I think you're going to see it as a mature sport, instead of a growth sport.

"We have to keep what we have healthy and build on it slowly. Maybe you can have a little bit of growth, but you're not going to have these huge 12 professional competitions and four skating events on every Saturday. It's going to be more realistic, probably where it should be," he states.

Perhaps this will even prove a beneficial regrouping period, offers former U.S. pair skater–turned–choreographer and director Lea Ann Miller.

"After the Tonya/Nancy saga, there was such a rush for skating, and everyone got a little greedy in the amount of competitions and shows that we did. I think it's time to take the opportunity, with the audience that we have, to do some quality programming and weed out some of the bad ideas or events and improve on the good ones," she proposes.

"Let's get the pro competitions back on the circuit and to a place where people can understand it. What's a pro event? What's a pro-am? Who's pro and who's amateur? It's very confusing for the public."

A nice idea, but the trick there is that pro skating needs to see a major upswing. As it stands now, fewer and fewer skaters are turning pro. The once fertile ground is near erosion. Two-time Olympic Ice Dance gold medalist Evgeny Platov once likened pro skating to the Titanic. "Maybe it's not sinking quite as fast, but it's sinking," he said.

Naturally, the predicament doesn't sit well at all with skating veterans who spent years and years building up their craft.

"Because of the changes in skating and the money the kids are making competing, there is no motivation for them to turn pro. When I competed, it was like I couldn't wait to not compete and break free from the chains and be a professional. A lot of us have talked about how it's bad that some of the skaters have no interest in being pro, because that's what really helps the sport to grow. We need a strong core of professionals who are doing something different," says Kristi Yamaguchi.

"It adds another dimension to skating besides competing. The sport needs that. As the established pros are getting older, we want to be able to pass the torch down to the younger ones, but not so many of them are turning pro."

Scott Hamilton and Paul Wylie feel the ISU is at the root of the professional vanishing act.

"I know that a lot of people in the ISU don't like professional skating. But without the balance of professional and competitive skating, I think the sport will be greatly harmed," declares Scott. "You can't put all your eggs in one basket."

Paul Wylie couldn't agree more.

"There existed a terrific balance between eligible skating and professional skating, even when they participated in events together. What's happened now is eligible skating has spread its wings, saying, 'We want all of this,' and there is no place for that new footing or that different style of competition. It has created somewhat of a crisis in our sport," he says.

"Skaters of my generation did not have to stop competing seriously when they turned professional, and that was a beautiful thing. But today, the only option for skaters who don't want to stop competing seriously is to stay in the ISU eligible competitions."

For the good of the sport, the ISU must recognize the situation, says Paul, and the solution to the dilemma lies within that organization.

"If the ISU wants to run a separate circuit, maybe that's the answer. They can engender something that is less restrictive, that is more conducive to the artistic growth of the skaters who are ready to leave the eligible ranks. One of the worst things that could happen is for skaters to just continue to hang out and compete in the same old competitions and continue to try to do a better and better short program and a better and better long program. What is going to wind up happening is the new skaters are just going to topple the once-champions, because they can't compete with them technically," he offers.

"It's impossible to grow by staying still, coloring within those lines, still using the same 2:40 and 4:30 programs. It's really important artistically for the skaters to expand their horizons and still compete, but to have a more freeing format."

Kain is of the same opinion, coming from a businessman's perspective. He notes that when the pro world was at its apex, so was the eligible world.

"The ISU and the USFSA need to deal with pro skating, as opposed to fighting it," he says. "They fought it back in the early 1980s, and then they kind of left it alone. Now, they're probably fighting more than helping it. They need to help it for their own sake, and I don't think they see that.

"We're trying to build individual athletes into as big of stars as they want to be. We're trying to get them to continue to improve their craft.

"The USFSA starts saying, we don't want anything competing with our events on ABC at all," he continues. "One way to do that is to squeeze out all other skating, so that the only skating you see is on ABC. But I think that's a real mistake for the sport, long term, and as the governing body for the sport, you can't be trying to squeeze the competition. You're supposed to be encouraging the competition. The more you get rid of competition, the more you're hurting your sport, because, clearly, every sport that's doing well has lots of different entities. So if they want to have this nice little package where they're the only game in town, they've basically, effectively, squeezed off the popularity of their own sport. People that are in that organization or whatever can get very narrow-minded and miss the plot."

Beyond the absence of a pro competitive circuit, Hamilton

fears for the survival of *Stars on Ice*—the tour he founded—without the frequent influx of new faces into pro skating.

"A show of *Stars on Ice* quality and significance really has a great impact on the entire sport and industry," he explains. "If something like that is unable to continue offering a high level of talent, because most of the skaters wanted to stay eligible or stay within the ISU structure exclusively, I think that the sport will really lose something. I sincerely hope that doesn't happen."

Perhaps ISU structure doesn't have to mean only Grand Prix and World competition. ISU President Ottavio Cinquanta has often spoken of the desire to add new formats for events. While his intention is keep everyone under the ISU umbrella, he acknowledges there need to be different styles of umbrellas.

"We prepare a new track," Cinquanta says. "This is the best solution, maybe, that there will be no more ineligible skaters.

"There will be entrepreneurs who will organize the events in cooperation with the ISU."

Along with available skaters, changing times and the economy pose real concerns to the major tours, *Stars on Ice* and *Champions on Ice*.

"I've never seen an Olympic tour not totally sold out," declares Brian Boitano, regarding the 2002 *Champions* show.

Randy Gardner predicts, "Over the next few years, what is going to sell will be very feel-good and family-oriented. That's what's happening with entertainment in general, because of what's going on in the world. We need that escapism."

Perfectly fitting the bill is Kenneth Feld's *Disney on Ice* tours. These story-driven productions, full of endearing characters and colorful, elaborate sets, transport an audience.

"We strive to give the customers what they want. We are constantly changing to stay up with the times and to make our shows better and more relevant," says Feld.

Between *Champions on Ice* and *Stars on Ice*, Gardner contends the former will have better luck with today's market.

"Going to see your favorite skating champion is a good departure, and Tommy's (*Champions*) tour offers that," Gardner says. "If you want to see Michelle Kwan and Sarah Hughes strut their stuff, you can do that there. There is and will be a market for that. And I don't think the people going there expect much else of that particular show. Now, when they go to *Stars on Ice*, which annually has a unique look, people expect every year the new production will top the prior one.

"I think this current tour for *Stars* will be really critical, because they're going to figure out the market. They can try and predict it, go out and see what's going on with the economy, but they won't know until they get out there. I think their team is very much top notch. It's trial and error."

While *Stars on Ice* producer Byron Allen is admittedly uncertain about how the next few years will play out, he thinks the tour's long-term future is bright—as long as Americans keep winning and are in the medals.

"Obviously, it's important there are North American champions in eligible skating who grow into popular figures, and I think that will continue," he says. "For the last 30 years, the U.S. has developed wonderful ladies' skaters, and certainly, since Scott Hamilton, they have had wonderful men's skaters. You have to believe that there will continue to be successful U.S. skaters, which will lead to interest in skating in general."

Lynn Plage, publicity director for *Champions on Ice*, believes that attitude won't propel the sport forward, as Russia and other countries continue to excel at figure skating, too.

"In order for figure skating to be a real success today, we have to embrace all the champions—Canadians, Russians, French, Americans, etc. We have to find a way for this to happen and for the sport as a whole to be embraced, not just the U.S. skaters," she insists.

Exactly who will lead skating as the new century marches on remains to be seen.

"Optimistically, I hope it's the skaters. If I have to be pessimistic, I'd say the ISU. I really feel that the ISU is compromised to the point where they can't be effective in figure skating," states Hamilton.

"It comes down to leadership. Whoever is leading the thing has to be effective and has to look at the big picture. There need to be some pretty tough decisions made over the next few years, including how they want to present their skaters, how often they present their skaters, the diversity of the sport and whether they're going to allow professional skating to really thrive.

"Skaters are pretty much going to have to take this thing and make it happen. I don't know who's going to be able to do that, but it's going to come out of a real love for the sport and integrity. You've got to put the sport first. And that's exactly what concerns me about the ISU: a lack of ownership of the issues and not putting the sport first. If they could do that, there would such a huge positive impact on the entire industry."

Rosenberg also questions the intent of skating's governing body. "I'm very disillusioned and depressed about [president] Cinquanta and the hierarchy of the ISU. It's almost like this present generation is going to have to die off before real change happens."

What figure skating needs most is a commissioner, says Hamilton.

"We need someone independent that can represent both

sides—the ISU and the skaters, as well as the professional and eligible ranks. This would be a huge step in the right direction for the sport."

However, Hamilton's not volunteering for the job. "I would hope that the commissioner would be somebody much smarter than I am," he laughs.

"But, whoever it is, I hope they love the sport as much as I do."

Epilogue
October 5, 2002
—Salt Lake City

G one were the fans.

Gone were the journalists.

Gone were the officials.

Gone were the stars.

As I walked past the Delta Center arena on this autumn day, while visiting friends in the host city of the 2002 XIX Olympic Winter Games, I felt like I was on an empty studio lot. No lights. No cameras. No action.

The sport of figure skating is entertainment.

With its larger-than-life personalities, no other sport in the world commands such physical discipline coupled with the ability to entertain like the sport of figure skating.

Figure skating so often mirrors Hollywood in all of its incarnations.

When the Hollywood studio system began to collapse in the 1950s with the invention of television, everyone at the time thought that movies would soon go by the wayside. While *Gone with the Wind* was certainly popular in 1939, it was later dwarfed in popularity by *Titanic* in 1997.

Figure skating is living its "1950s" at the start of the 21st century.

When figure skating began its rise in popularity in the late 1980s, who would have believed that the 1990s would have seen it become a quarter-billion dollar industry?

But unlike Hollywood, which was able to see a new light, it is unlikely that some of the powers that be in figure skating see that clearly. Although reforms are coming from the ISU in terms of rule changes, the damage has already been done. Both skaters and fans are resisting these changes, as they are neither substantial nor truly meaningful. Rather, the forthcoming changes are superficial.

Hard decisions need to be made, and they need to be made by those who matter. There is only one group in this industry of figure skating that can make a difference.

The skaters.

While the Hamiltons, Witts, Boitanos and Yamaguchis of our great sport continue to be involved, they know that the torch must pass to a younger generation—a generation that understands what building something means. A generation that is not scared to say "no." A generation that is willing to take a stand and to make a difference.

For it is the Kwans, Yagudins, Stojkos and Hughes' who need to take command. Decisions do not need to be made in the board-room of a television network or congress hall, they need to be made on the ice.

The relationships the skaters have amongst themselves are unique only to them. It doesn't matter if you are a publisher, producer, agent, official or judge. You may be with them, but you are not one of them. The old guard needs to understand this, and the new administrators need to work with this.

The sport of figure skating will endure, because it is a tapestry of cultures from almost every nation on earth. While the skaters have a commonality amongst themselves, all of those who work in the sport speak a common language that can effect true progress and development when working towards a singular goal.

Figure skating needs that one common purpose to bring a new order to the sport that culminates in popularity and diversification.

Do we all not remember the creation of The World Professional Figure Skating Championships or The Grand Prix of Figure Skating? That is what those in figure skating do best. They create and cater to the drive of the amateurs and the brilliance of the professionals.

Luminaries such as the Dick Buttons and Dorothy Hamills have done their performances for king and country both on and off the ice. While they continue to contribute with great passion, it was their innate ability to create, perform and compete that shaped the modern world of figure skating and instilled in others the excitement to propel the sport forward into the 21st century and beyond.

For this is the sport of figure skating.

Until the next performance.

Credits

Photography
Andrew Shapter, Don Snyder, Michael Bernadsky,
Bryan Helm, Patrick O'Connor, Rebecca Patrick,
Cindy Dupre, Vicki Luy, Christina Bunn,
Kelly Behning and J. Barry Mittan

Copy Editing
Tammy Kaehler

INDEX

A

Acrobats, The, 112, 127
Allen, Byron, 27, 90, 119, 279
Anissina, Marina, 154, 229, 242-245
Averbukh, Ilia, 154, 243

B

Babilonia, Tai, 31, 61, 148, 222, 237, 249
Bach, Thomas, 244
Baiul, Oksana, 3, 16, 49, 52, 76, 77, 90, 99, 100, 117, 163, 166, 174-185
Balkov, Yuki, 243
Bayer, Jennifer, 127
Bechke, Elena, 31, 138, 230, 236, 263
Berezhnaya, Elena, 17, 24, 25, 49, 74, 75, 77, 227, 229, 230-239, 245
Besedin, Vladimir, see Acrobats
Bezic, Sandra, 9, 29, 32, 38, 87-89, 131, 201, 229
Biellmann, Denise, 153
Bill Graham Productions, 86
Billings, Jef, 41, 88
Billington, Ken, 87
Blalock, Jane, 172
Blumberg, Judy, 85
Bobek, Nicole, 81, 113
Boitano, Brian, 8, 9, 15, 31, 32, 36, 49, 51, 59, 73, 85-87, 92,

104, 117-120, 125, 149, 150, 159, 161, 165, 214, 265, 272, 273, 278
Bonaly, Surya, 13
Borg, Bjorn, 83
Bourne, Shae-Lynn, 25, 154, 245
Bowman, Christopher, 30
Brasseur, Isabelle, 76, 128
Brennan, Christine, 197, 198
Browning, Kurt, 17, 28-31, 51, 52, 59, 60, 92, 100, 107, 118-120, 203
Burg, Michael, 117, 131, 187, 202, 273
Button, Dick, 2, 24, 84, 97, 98, 100-103, 116-123, 285

C

Callaghan, Richard, 192, 194
Candeloro, Philippe, 26, 126, 234, 235, 241
Candid Productions, 98, 100, 101, 116, 118, 121, 122
Carlisle, Michael, 77, 176-180
Carlisle, Peter, 183
Carroll, Frank, 217-219
Carruthers
    Kitty & Peter, 85
    Peter, 166
Chait
    Boris, 246, 248
    Galit, 228, 246, 247
Chidlow, Marilyn, 140, 141
Cichy, Craig, 101, 102, 121, 122
Cinquanta, Ottavio, 14, 119, 133, 141-144, 243, 254, 257, 258, 261, 278, 280
Cohen, Sasha, 80, 157

Collins
    Michael, 75, 108
    Tom, 3, 13, 14, 49, 51, 71-85, 91, 127, 178-180, 204, 223
Collins Marshall Management (CMM), 82, 108
Correa, Rob, 116
Cousins, Robin, 104-106, 130
Cranston, Toller, 8, 12, 24, 82, 92

D

Dean, Christopher, 18, 25, 28, 52, 85, 88-91, 154, 232, 248
Decker, Mary, 12
Dijkhuizen, Eric-Paul, 130, 131
Disney, 11, 12, 38, 128, 129, 164, 211-213, 278
Disson, Steve, 13, 14, 91, 103-108
Dore, David, 261, 262
Drobiazko, Margarita, 228, 246

E

Eisler, Lloyd, 76, 128, 225, 236, 266
Elbe, Erin, 207
Eldredge, Todd, 74, 77, 92, 107, 118-120, 193, 194
Evert, Chris, 198

F

Faulkner, Megan, 193
Feld, Kenneth, 12, 128-131, 278, 279
Fenech, Craig, 17, 49, 50, 75
Ference, Brad, 216
Ferguson, Claire, 121
Fleming, Peggy, 27, 83
Fusar-Poli, Barbara, 154, 265

Futerman, Ed, 138

G
Gailhaguet, Didier, 138, 228, 241, 244, 245
Galindo, Rudy, 11, 33, 74, 81
Gardner, Randy, 61, 78-80, 149, 153, 170, 278, 279
Goebel, Timothy, 151, 152
Goldberg, Shep, 64, 212
Gordeeva, Ekaterina (Katia), 31, 38, 39, 48, 51, 57, 58, 90-92, 232, 233, 235
Graham, Bill, 86
Greenwood, Jack, 140, 141
Gregorian, Irina, 112, 127
Grinkov, Sergei, 38-40, 58, 232

H
Hamilton, Scott, 5, 7-10, 13, 26-28, 31, 35, 40, 51, 83-85, 89-92, 104, 105, 123, 124, 148, 156-159, 169, 197, 203, 222, 227, 229, 253, 261, 264, 266, 269-281
Harding, Tonya, 100, 116, 119, 163, 275
Harper, Dianne, 213, 214
Hartshorn, Anita, 126
Heath, Craig, 129, 130
Hedican, Bret, 33, 62
Henie, Sonja, 72
Hollander, Dan, 127, 128
Howard, Phyllis, 135, 136, 215, 257-259
Hughes, Sarah, 41-45, 64, 65, 157, 168, 201, 211, 212, 220, 222, 258
Hula-Hoop Girl, see Gregorian, Irina

I

Ina, Kyoko, 237

International Management Group (IMG), 3, 11, 13, 38, 46, 47, 50, 69, 71, 72, 77, 82-92, 97, 100, 106, 107, 112-115, 131, 205, 274, see also Kain, Bob

International Skating Union (ISU), 2, 14, 72, 98, 119-123, 133, 140-144, 149, 153-155, 228, 229, 234, 241, 243, 244, 247-249, 254-257, 261-265, 268, 276, 278, 280, 281

J

Jefferson Pilot Sports, 98-100, 103, 131

Jenner, Bruce, 150

Jones, Courtney, 248

K

Kadavy, Caryn, 116

Kain, Bob, 11, 69, 72, 82-85, 90-92, 107, 274, 277

Kawahara, Sarah, 35, 79, 217

Kelly, Gene, 28

Kerrigan, Nancy, 16, 44, 67, 76, 100, 116, 119, 126, 131, 159, 163-174, 178-180, 220, 221, 275

Kirk, Jennifer, 63, 64

Kostomarov, Roman, 248

Kraatz, Victor, 154, 230, 245, 263, 264

Kresge, Karen, 87

Kulik, Ilia, 46, 47, 48, 55, 58, 77, 78, 90, 118, 124, 148, 149, 152, 153, 234, 273

Kunz, Wolfgang, 140

Kwan
    Danny, 220
    Michelle, 11, 12, 40-43, 58, 59, 64, 65, 76, 79, 119, 137,

138, 148, 157, 159, 195-202, 209-224, 258, 274, 284

Kwiatkowski, Tonia, 112, 126

L
Lakernik, Alexander, 142, 244
Lang, Naomi, 247
LeGougne, Marie-Reine, 138, 228, 237, 241, 243, 244, 264
LeFevre, John, 136, 137
Lendl, Ivan, 167
Leno, Jay, 235
Lipinski
    Pat and Jack, 189-207
    Tara, 16, 52, 60, 77, 89, 90, 99, 107, 117-119, 189-207, 214, 219, 222
Lobacheva, Irina, 154, 243
Lodato, Francis (Frank), 174, 178-185
Lopez, Jennifer, 59
Lynn, Janet, 82

M
Manilow, Barry, 115
Manley, Liz, 13, 17, 237, 256, 264
Manning, Peyton, 172
Marco Entertainment, 98
Margaglio, Maurizio, 265
Marinin, Maxim, 237
Marshall, Lee, 95, 98, 99, 102, 108
Martini, Paul, 262
Maurizi, Craig, 193
Mendenhall, Mike, 213

Meno, Jenni, 256
Miller, Lea Ann, 14, 29, 87, 105, 206, 230-232, 236, 266, 275
Millot, Eric, 112, 125
Mimms, Lee, 83
Mishin, Alexei, 75
Moskvina, Tamara, 17, 24, 25, 74, 75, 230-233, 238, 244

N
Navka, Tatiana, 247
Navratilova, Martina, 198
Nichol, Lori, 215-218, 231
Nicks, John, 232, 236, 267
Nikolaev, Valentin, 176, 182

O
O'Donnell, Rosie, 235
Ogden, Jay, 72, 82, 83
Ohno, Apolo Anton, 221
Orser, Brian, 9, 10, 14, 28, 46, 52, 85-89, 114-120, 139, 149, 150, 153, 185, 230, 235, 255, 256, 271

P
Palmer, Dick, 86
Peizerat, Gwendal, 64, 154, 155, 229, 242-244, 266
Pelletier, David, 16, 17, 29, 48-51, 60, 61, 66, 75, 159, 225-240, 255
Petrenko, Viktor, 76, 128, 175, 179
Petrov, Denis, 33
Piseev, Valetin, 77
Plage, Lynn, 25, 62, 122, 279, 280
Platov, Evgeny, 275

Plushenko, Evǵeni, 128, 151
Polishuk, Alexei, see Acrobats
Pound, Dick, 244

R
Rand, Jeb, 127
Rather, Dan, 233
Roca, Renée, 247
Rogers, Sharon, 247
Rosenberg, Michael, 18, 23, 46, 76-80, 93, 97-99, 103, 143,
    182, 272, 280
Ruh, Lucinda, 13, 113, 114

S
Sabovcik, Jozef, 125
Saegusa, Yuki, 115
Sakhnovksy, Sergey, 228, 246
Salé, Jamie, 16, 17, 28, 49-51, 60, 61, 66, 75, 159, 227-240
Sampras, Pete, 167
Sato, Yuka, 113, 114
Scotvold
    Evy, 173
    Mary, 173
Seibert, Michael, 85, 88, 273, 274
Senft, Jean, 243
SFX, 99, 100, 101, 118
Shaw, Ann, 140, 141, 144, 248
Sikharulidze, Anton, 17, 24, 25, 49, 74, 75, 77, 227-230, 232,
    234, 238, 239, 245
Slater, Nicky, 104-106
Slutskaya, Irina, 41, 65, 258

Solomon, Jerry, 44, 131, 132, 159, 160, 166, 168-171, 174, 222
Stapleford, Sally, 142-144, 228, 244, 260, 261, 263-265
Sterling, Michael, 27, 28, 45, 47, 48
Stojko, Elvis, 26, 29, 51, 52, 119, 126, 137, 138
Sumners, Rosalynn (Roz), 8, 11, 12, 15, 39, 42, 83, 85, 116, 138, 145, 157-160, 206, 233, 274
Sunik, Eugene (Gene), 183, 184
Swain, Gary, 205
Sweiding, Frank, 126

T
Tchernyshev, Peter, 247
Tokhtakhounov, Alimzhan, 2, 17, 229, 241, 242, 245
Tom Collins Enterprises, see Collins, Tom
Torvill, Jayne, 85
Totmianina, Tatiana, 237

U
Underhill, Barbara, 262
United States Figure Skating Association (USFSA), 73, 78, 98, 104, 107, 108, 120-123, 135-138, 149, 212, 258, 261,277
Urmanov, Alexei, 26

V
Vanagas, Povilas, 156, 228, 246
Vogel, Synde, 191

W
Wagner, Robin, 41, 43, 44, 65, 205, 214
Weiss, Michael, 151, 251, 256, 262, 267

Witt, Katarina, 9, 10, 15, 21, 35-38, 51, 52, 85, 87, 89, 99, 115-117, 150, 152, 159, 165, 174
Woods, Tiger, 17
Wright, Benjamin, 139, 142, 262, 263
Wylie, Paul, 15, 19, 26, 27, 29-32, 39, 40, 114, 119, 173, 231, 234-236, 255, 256, 260, 261, 264, 276

Y

Yagudin, Alexei, 40, 45, 46, 48, 62, 63, 75, 92, 118, 120, 151, 152, 158, 234, 255
Yamaguchi, Kristi, 10, 11, 15, 27, 32-35, 46, 52, 62, 89, 92, 105, 107, 109, 115, 119, 159, 160, 168, 221, 269-281

Z

Zhulin, Alexander, 247
Zimmerman, John, 16, 35, 233, 234, 237, 249
Zmievskaya, Galina, 77, 175-178